American Silhouettes

American Silhouettes

RHETORICAL IDENTITIES OF THE FOUNDERS

ALBERT FURTWANGLER

YALE UNIVERSITY PRESS

NEW HAVEN AND LONDON

Designed by Sally Harris
and set in Fournier type
by Huron Valley Graphics, Inc.
Printed in the United States of America by
Vail-Ballou Press, Binghamton, N.Y.

Library of Congress Cataloging-in-Publication Data

Furtwangler, Albert, 1942–
American silhouettes.

Includes index.
1. United States—Politics and government—1783–1809.
2. Politicians—United States—History—18th century.
3. Statesmen—United States—History—18th century.
4. United States—Constitutional history.   I. Title.
E303.F87 1987   973.4   86-23424
ISBN 0-300-03798-8 (cloth)
0-300-04501-8 (pbk.)

"The Spectator's Apprentice" is adapted from "Franklin's Apprenticeship
and the Spectator," which originally appeared in The New England Quarterly.
"Cato at Valley Forge" originally appeared in Modern Language Quarterly
in somewhat different form.

The paper in this book meets the guidelines for
permanence and durability of the Committee on
Production Guidelines for Book Longevity
of the Council on Library Resources.

3   5   7   9   10   8   6   4   2

Contents

Preface

This book is a study of early American political leaders and the cultural ideals they reshaped in creating the Constitution. As a result it treats matters that lie outside what I usually teach in literature courses at a Canadian university. But rhetoric is a subject that necessarily overlaps other specialized fields, and at many turns I have had the good fortune to find an expert guide just when I needed one.

Chapters 2 and 4 evolved from questions about the influence of Joseph Addison in America. Early versions appeared in *New England Quarterly* (1979) and *Modern Language Quarterly* (1980) and were improved by the helpful advice of the editors of those journals.

In 1977–78 I spent a sabbatical year as a visiting Fellow at Yale. There I began a book about the *Federalist* papers, *The Authority of Publius* (1984). I tried to see what "Publius," the supposed author, had to say about the Constitution, apart from what Hamilton or Madison might have argued. That work led directly to the later conflict between Hamilton as "Pacificus" and Madison as "Helvidius." At the same time I attended a history seminar taught by Barbara A. Black on constitutionalism and the American Revolution. The students in that course were particularly alert and able that semester; I remain grateful to them as well as their instructor for a lively approach to the complex legal ideas of John Adams and John Marshall. I also wish to thank Leslie Brisman of the Yale English department for supporting my work in New Haven throughout the year.

In 1984–85 I spent another sabbatical year as a member of the Institute for Advanced Study in Princeton. I was given an office just a few steps away from Morton White, who was pursuing similar interests in early American political thought. He set me a good example and from time to time provided direct help in solving particular problems. The year at the Institute made it possible for me to complete this manuscript.

Jay Fliegelman of Stanford University read the entire work with a sharp eye for detail and tone, and pointed out many possible relations with other recent studies.

All these experts in law, literature, philosophy, and cultural history have saved me from glaring errors, but it is only right to insist that I am responsible for remaining flaws of fact, interpretation, and proportion.

At Mount Allison University I have had the benefit of a good college library; Anne Ward deserves special mention for locating some obscure titles for me and obtaining them from far away. I have also been served promptly and well by librarians at Yale University, Princeton University, the Institute for Advanced Study, and the Historical Society of Pennsylvania. Money for ongoing research has been provided from the faculty research fund at Mount Allison and the Marjorie Young Bell Faculty Fund.

My wife and I have a pact: we do not read each other's manuscripts. But her work as a writer has strengthened mine, and her daily conversation and support have brightened many of these pages.

Trumbull's Group Portrait

One of the most familiar images of the American founding is *The Declaration of Independence* by John Trumbull. This painting has been so widely reproduced that most educated Americans have seen it often and recognize it at once. A full-size version hangs in the Rotunda of the Capitol, and smaller reproductions have served as illustrations or frontispieces in scores of books. It has even circulated in ordinary life: it graced the back of the two-dollar bill and was a postage stamp design. All this would certainly have gratified Trumbull, for he intended to memorialize a great event for millions of viewers. He tried carefully to recapture the faces of the men who established the new nation—not only John Adams, Thomas Jefferson, and Benjamin Franklin who stand out here, but most of the other members of the 1776 Congress. In an age before photography, he crossed an ocean and rode hundreds of miles to make likenesses of these men before they died. Here, as well as a patriotic American artist could render it, is a group portrait of forty-eight Americans at the moment of their emergence into a new national identity.

This painting has been the subject of much learned discussion because of its place among the works of a pioneer American artist. But *The Declaration* also deserves a careful look from anyone interested in political history. It presents an intriguing vision of the establishment of a new political order; of an act of self-determination; of a declaration of principles shared and endorsed by a large deliberative assembly; and of a few men singled out because of their special talents for composing such a document. The painting helps us remember this scene with full recognition of its main elements. As a historical painting, however, it effectiveness depends on the viewer's knowing more than is shown. We must recall the meaning it depicts and see Franklin, Adams, and Jefferson anew as they lay their common declaration out for thoughtful approval.

Trumbull's work on this painting was colored by his own involvement in the Revolution. His career as an artist was inseparable from his identity as a revolutionary soldier and American agent abroad.[1] Trumbull was the son of Governor Jonathan Trumbull of Connecticut, the only colonial governor to side with the revolutionaries and remain in office during the war. His father and older brother organized supplies for Washington's armies, and young Trumbull himself was soon in uniform. His sketches of fortifications around Boston drew him to Washington's attention and he became the general's second aide-de-camp. Within a few months he had attained a colonel's rank; but a delay of his commission meant a loss in seniority, and after some angry letters to Congress, he resigned. In 1780 he made his way to London and the studio of Benjamin West. But in wartime Trumbull was conspicuous as an American in England, and soon after the hanging of Major John André as a British spy, he was arrested and kept in prison for over seven months. Many years later he again served his country in a time of crisis; from 1794 to 1804 he was a diplomatic agent in Europe. At the outbreak of the French Revolution he had carried messages from Lafayette to President Washington; during the 1790s he carried secret diplomatic messages in and out of Paris. He felt he narrowly escaped being arrested by Tallyrand during the XYZ affair in 1797. Meanwhile, Trumbull found a way of combining his artistic ambitions with a practical scheme for gaining an income. In England Benjamin West and John Singleton Copley were becoming well-known for their historical paintings of recent heroic scenes. West had realized a great profit through

1. Details about Trumbull's life and art are derived from his own account and from three modern studies: *The Autobiography of Colonel John Trumbull,* ed. Theodore Sizer (New Haven: Yale University Press, 1953); Irma B. Jaffe, *John Trumbull: Patriot-Artist of the American Revolution* (Boston: New York Graphic Society, 1975) and *Trumbull: The Declaration of Independence* (New York: Viking, 1976); and Helen A. Cooper, ed., *John Trumbull: The Hand and Spirit of a Painter* (New Haven: Yale University Art Gallery, 1982).

the engraving of his painting, *The Battle of La Hogue,* and Trumbull saw an opportunity uniquely suited to his own talents. By creating a series of small paintings of the American Revolution and marketing engravings from them, he hoped to reach a wide audience in America and even gain commissions from the government.

By 1785 he had enough faith in this scheme to propose it to his brothers and seek their financial backing. He had already begun *The Death of General Warren at the Battle of Bunker's Hill,* the first of five designs he had in mind. The earliest of these paintings were to show the dignity of noble combat through the dramatic deaths of military heroes. Later paintings were to show the end of hostilities in a magnanimous capture and two formal surrenders. The eight paintings that Trumbull finally produced encompassed a variety of moods and settings: battles at Bunker's Hill, Quebec, Trenton, and Princeton; surrenders at Saratoga and Yorktown; and congressional scenes in Philadelphia and Annapolis. The execution of this plan was to occupy Trumbull's thoughts and energies, off and on, for the next forty years. In America he had trouble finding subscribers to the series; in Europe he suffered long delays in getting his first two panels engraved. He had to turn to portrait commissions, trading ventures, and other employments in order to support himself and stay ahead of his creditors.

In a 1789 letter to Jefferson, Trumbull claimed that this project of paintings and engravings represented a special vocation. His aims, he wrote, were "to diffuse the knowledge and preserve the Memory of the noblest series of Actions which have ever dignified the History of Man." And he saw himself as a man singled out to perform this task:

Some superiority also arose from my having borne personally, an humble part in the great Events which I was to describe:—no one lives possessing with me this advantage, and none can come after me to divide the Honor of Truth and Authenticity, however easily I may be exceeded in Elegance:—Vanity was thus on the side of Duty, and while I felt some honest pride in the prospect of performing a work such as had never been done before, and in which it was not easy to see that I should ever have a successful Rival:—I flatterd myself that, in devoting a few Years of my Life to this Object, I did not make

John Trumbull, *The Declaration of Independence*
Copyright Yale University Art Gallery

an absolute waste of Time, or squander uselessly, talents from which my Country might justly have demanded more valuable Services.[2]

With these words Trumbull turned down an attractive, well-paid appointment as Jefferson's secretary in Paris. He returned to America to gather subscriptions and to locate and draw the subjects of his works in progress. This credo (often repeated in various forms) helped him continue his project for decades to come.

It is difficult to know how sincere Trumbull was in his patriotic zeal. He was a proud, ambitious man, and in passages like this one, the reader can detect strains of self-importance and defensiveness. Being "Colonel Trumbull," the "patriot-artist," as he styled himself, was his way of being more than a mere artisan. His family had tried to dissuade him from a precarious and menial career. In Europe he might be dismissed (or persecuted) as a mere American. In America he might starve or be patronized by prosperous citizens with limited taste. But by working at a great series of public prints, he could convince at least himself that he was engaged in a high calling, one worthy of his distinguished birth and arduous training. In the end his persistence paid off. In 1817 he at last received a commission to design paintings for the Capitol; he contributed to the plan of the Rotunda where four of his Revolution panels remain enshrined.

In any case, what matters about Trumbull's career and expressed aims is how they affect *The Declaration*—how he might have seen the historical moment he depicts. In his series of eight panels on the Revolution, this one is a striking exception. The others all show military actions or heroes; here all the figures are civilians. The others are full of color or drama; this one is still and somber. The others show armies and heroes that might have participated in any conflict. They are paintings fully comparable to works by Copley or West or to Trumbull's own scenes from other wars. But *The Declaration* and *The Resignation of General Washington* (designed as a companion piece to *The Declaration*) present uniquely American subjects. *The Declaration* is therefore not only the most famous of Trumbull's paintings but the one that may justify his own exalted claims.

---

2. Trumbull to Jefferson, June 11, 1789, in *The Papers of Thomas Jefferson*, ed. Julian P. Boyd (Princeton: Princeton University Press, 1958), 15:177. Trumbull gave a different version of this letter in his *Autobiography*, pp. 158–62.

The painting needs to be seen in several lights, some of which may mislead a casual viewer. At one level, for example, it provokes commentary about Trumbull's technical competence. One can see in it the influence of West and Copley or his own possible influence on later painters like Jacques-Louis David. Or the several finished versions and engravings can be compared to evaluate Trumbull's talents and limitations in managing proportion, light, color, space, and the arrangement in classic poses of the central figures. These observations place Trumbull as a professional but not entirely original eighteenth-century artist.

At another level, the picture should be judged against the claim that it is an exact copy of a historic scene. This is a point that Trumbull encourages in his own commentaries: "To preserve the resemblace of the men who were the authors of this memorable act, was an essential object of this painting." And again: "Nothing has been neglected by the artist, that was in his power, to render this a faithful memorial of the great event."[3] Trumbull made careful lists of the members of Congress in 1776 and traveled from London to Paris and New York, and from New Hampshire to South Carolina, to make his sketches. He claimed to be scrupulous about details of clothing, furnishings, and the room itself. But the painting has drawn dozens of carping comments about his errors. Some of his figures cannot be clearly identified. His chairs seem to be French rather than American. The back wall actually had one door, not two, and probably had no flags mounted on it. The windows should have venetian blinds, not heavy draperies. The actual business of Congress could not have looked like this nor could it have been viewed from this point in the chamber. These are familiar observations about the painting contradicting Trumbull's claims to verisimilitude.

But at a third level, this scene of historical figures is warmed by Trumbull's patriotism and his personal acquaintance with its subjects. He went out of his way to see these faces—to observe them closely and bring them together again on canvas. As it happened, he knew or came to know many of them very well. Of the main figures in the foreground, from left to right, for example: John Adams was minister to Britain after the war, and Trumbull saw him often in London; Adams had also been a contemporary at

3. John Trumbull, "Catalogue of Paintings by Colonel Trumbull," in *Autobiography, Reminiscences and Letters by John Trumbull from 1756 to 1841* (New Haven, 1841), pp. 416, 418.

Harvard of Trumbull's oldest brother, Joseph. Roger Sherman was Governor Trumbull's ally in mobilizing Connecticut's resources for war on the eve of the Revolution; Trumbull's brother was elected as Sherman's alternate to the Continental Congress of 1774. Robert R. Livingston was a wealthy New Yorker with a taste for fine arts, as well as a national leader and international negotiator; he founded the American Academy of the Arts, of which Trumbull became a forceful member after 1805. Thomas Jefferson befriended Trumbull in Paris, relied on him to carry his letters to Maria Cosway, and made a sketch of the floor plan of the meeting room in Independence Hall; Trumbull's first sketch of *The Declaration of Independence* is on the same sheet of paper.[4] Benjamin Franklin had been the American commissioner in Paris in 1780 and had sent Trumbull to London with a letter of introduction to Benjamin West. And John Hancock was the president of Congress who urged young Trumbull to tone down his protests about his delayed military commission.

Trumbull visited under many of these men's roofs and reminisced with them. As a portrait artist, he could be ingratiating, drawing a subject out and quickly capturing the result. His portrait of *Washington at the Battle of Trenton* (1792), for example, was widely regarded as a fine likeness of the revolutionary general. Trumbull reports: "I told the President my object; he entered into it warmly, and, as the work advanced, we talked of the scene, its dangers, its almost desperation. He *looked* the scene again, and I happily transferred to the canvass, the lofty expression of his animated countenance, the high resolve to conquer or to perish" (*Autobiography,* p. 171). In the original version of *The Declaration* Jefferson's head is so lifelike that Maria Cosway begged Trumbull to make her a copy, which she cherished. Although not all of Trumbull's portraits were so successful, painting small lifelike heads was one of his gifts. When Goethe saw *Bunker's Hill* at the engraver's, he remarked, "His talent is evident particularly in the character portraits achieved in bold strokes."[5] And a recent critic has argued that Trumbull's miniature studies for the historical paintings were "serious attempts to document the character as well as the likeness" of the early patriots; they are "the most beautiful and sophisti-

---

4. This sheet is reproduced in Cooper, p. 79, and in Jaffe, *John Trumbull,* p. 105.
5. Goethe to Schiller, August 30, 1797, quoted in Jaffe, *John Trumbull,* p. 316.

cated portraits" that were painted in America at that time.[6] Trumbull's achievement was a result not only of hard-won artistic skill but of attention and devotion to his subjects.

Finally, on still another level, *The Declaration* can be seen as an example of Trumbull's other great talent, that of historical composition. He reconstructed the event not as a camera would have caught it but as a painter with an eye for its enduring value, its political significance.

The painting presents the actions of three, perhaps four interrelated orders of men. In the background are general members of Congress. Some can be identified readily; others are and were so obscure that keys to the painting were long unquestioned, even though they were wrong. At the center of the room stands the five-member committee that drafted the declaration. Two of its members—Sherman and Livingston—are partly obscured by the others, who stand out distinctly. John Adams appears in full length in a brown suit, at the center of the painting. Jefferson, wearing a bright red waistcoat, places the document on the table; taller than anyone in the group, he also stands well forward. Immediately beside him is Franklin, whose torso is conspicuously heavy and dark and whose eyes gaze over the head of the president whom the others seem to address. In the foreground to the right are the president and secretary, Hancock and Charles Thomson, the one seated in an armchair filling the lower right corner, the other, almost as tall as Jefferson, standing next to the central table. Both of these figures, in formal black and wearing wigs, are turned so that we see their expressionless profiles. Together with the members of the committee these two officers form a circle at the front of the room around the table, with the rest of Congress forming a semicircle around them.

This arrangement, then, shows Congress witnessing its own act. The committee seems to have just come forward from seats among the others, recalling the fact that they arose from equal membership among the various state delegations. Similarly, the president and secretary are distinguished from the others (who are seated, or at tables, or standing around the room) mainly by their formal dress. This is evidently not the moment of signing the declaration, but of the committee's laying it on the table in late June among the other books and papers of Congress. The attention of

6. Oswaldo Rodriguez Roque, "Trumbull's Portraits," in Cooper, p. 101.

the room is directed to this presentation: what has this committee brought forward? The picture thus is true to the title of the paper Jefferson holds in his hands: "A Declaration by the Representatives of the United States of America, in General Congress Assembled." It was not Jefferson who made the declaration, though he penned this draft. It was not the committee, though they amended it. Nor did the individual signers create it, by dint of their personal signatures. Rather, it was the "Representatives . . . of the United States . . . in General Congress Assembled." As well as it can be portrayed, this is Congress in the *act* of declaring—attending to a draft it has requested of the committee and that it will adopt after consideration and refinement.

In declaring independence from Britain, Congress also declared itself the central government of a new America. The members pledged to each other their "lives, fortunes, and sacred honor." They also pledged their states to joint enterprises of war and peace—all under the direction of this Congress. The states had already been acting through Congress to support armies in the field and to name a commander in chief. But until independence was declared, Congress was an extralegal body, merely coordinating the efforts of various state rebellions. Hereafter it would not be extralegal but the center of American legality. And the painting seems to reflect these men's conscious choice of this interdependence.

They appear to be soberly prepared for answering only to one another. Their president is not a splendid royal governor, but one member elected by the others. The committee is not an intermediary council or a band of aristocrats, but a distinguished group of men acting for and among their fellows. In fact, this scene would probably have had much the same meaning if, in history, the personalities had been transposed. There would still have been a declaration if Franklin had happened to sit in Hancock's chair or if, say, George Clinton, John Witherspoon, George Wythe, Elbridge Gerry, and Robert Morris had brought the paper forward. The somber, dull colors; the attentive faces; the bare walls and floors, and the simple furnishings; the lack of finished detail on the doors and windows— all bespeak democratic plainness in a modern act of daring that brought forth the American Republic.

A fourth order of men is conspicuously absent here—the brilliantly clad soldiers who fill Trumbull's other paintings. There is a display of captured

British colors, but hanging in a faded symmetrical pattern in the background. In part these flags point up the importance of what is happening in this plain room. The declaration means national war; it spells violence and upheaval for people in every state and the threat of punishment for treason in the event of defeat. In part these trophies also suggest high optimism: the British have lost these banners and will lose more. As Trumbull knew, glorious flags and uniforms filled many other scenes. But in this one the central action is peaceful, sheltered deliberation. The members look away from the flags; even the president, who faces the back wall, cannot see them, for his view is blocked by the committee.

This reading of the painting is corroborated by the final work in Trumbull's series. *The Resignation of General Washington* is a companion piece and balance to *The Declaration.* Here Washington stands tall in the center of the room among a group of uniformed officers, tendering another document to the president. The president of Congress is again seated behind a table; beside him is the same towering figure of Charles Thomson, the secretary; the members of Congress are arranged in a circle; the walls and floors are bare. But in this scene the president and secretary are on the viewer's left; if the two pictures are set side by side, these officers of Congress appear in almost the same postures, but back to back. Congress is arranged here to look in a different direction—to receive Washington's entourage, accèpt his resignation, and witness his return to private life. On the back wall of this chamber there are no trophies of war; instead lady spectators surround Martha Washington on a balcony. In a moment Congress will resume its regular business after Washington has passed through the domestic portal on the right. Trumbull's sequence thus ends in another celebration of congressional authority. The war, even though it lasted eight years, was only an episode in the establishment of an enduring independent civilian government.[7]

After careful analysis, however, *The Declaration* remains a puzzling picture. Its focus constantly shifts. It seems to preserve a moment in history, a concerted action by a roomful of like-minded men. Yet it also preserves the distinctive characteristics of dozens of individuals. Like many histori-

---

7. There is a sharp note here in the fact that Washington tenders his resignation to Thomas Mifflin, who became president of Congress after being Washington's subordinate and later his active critic and enemy. Trumbull was Washington's second aide-de-camp; Mifflin was the first.

John Trumbull, *Resignation of General Washington*
Copyright Yale University Art Gallery

ans of this period, Trumbull seems caught between two aims: one to generalize, to see a common purpose reducing these congressmen to tiny elements in a grand design; the other to particularize, to preserve for posterity the exact lineaments of each face. This double focus leaves us with questions about the central characters in the scene. Most of the faces are turned toward the committee presenting the declaration. Among them, Adams, Jefferson, and Franklin stand out—not only as representative statesmen but as distinctive men, costumed in different colors. What did Trumbull see in each individual? What did he understand about this new alliance of a Bostonian, a Philadelphian, and a Virginian? What, in his mind, was their relationship to Washington, who dominates in his other paintings? What did he want us to recognize and remember about these men?

The chapters to follow recall some of Trumbull's methods, but in a different form. I have organized a series of inter-related scenes or chapters of the Revolution and early constitutional period. But instead of examining faces and postures, I have studied the founders' words. I have tried to represent not how they looked but how they composed formal identities in print and asked to be read by their countrymen. Accordingly, I call these chapters "silhouettes," or portraits in paper. But that term carries some connotations, too, which I should explain from the outset.

A silhouette is a portrait traced from the shadow (usually in profile) of a living person. Often the tracing is done on black paper and then cut out and mounted on a light background. The idea is very old; shadow pictures are a primitive form of art. But the great period of paper silhouettes was the eighteenth and early nineteenth centuries—from the time that paper became plentiful and cheap to the advent of photography. These works were simple. Anyone with a bit of dexterity, a pencil, and scissors might turn out a rough likeness. There were also itinerant portrait takers who made shadow pictures professionally. Some had various "machines" that cast a steady shadow and reduced the size of the tracing by means of a pantograph. Other artists with skills as sharp as their scissors could snip out a likeness quickly and directly—sometimes of a single bust, sometimes of full-length figures and groups.

In any case, a well-executed silhouette can have a haunting effect. Although the art lies in firm, decisive cutting, the result seems inartistic and ephemeral—the passing shadow of a mortal being. Some figures seem to outline a general type; others, to be the prints of unique individuals. Both extremes are well represented by eighteenth-century examples. Around 1775 silhouettes were gathered into a catalog of character types by Johann Kaspar Lavater and circulated widely to illustrate his popular theories of physiognomy.[8] On the other hand, some silhouettes recorded the odd or the illustrious. Jonathan Swift, early in the century, wrote a mocking poem about an odd face: "On Dan Jackson's Picture Cut in Paper." In the same spirit Major André made silhouettes of his fellow officers. And in a more reverent mood, Nelly Custis tried her hand at capturing the likenesses of her grandparents, George and Martha Washington.[9] Hers was an example of silhouettes conveying both the general and the particular. By producing what one author has called "shades of our ancestors," the silhouette maker traces the distinctive profile of a forebear and by implication records a lineage of common features.

All these associations suit my attempts here to trace identities projected by Franklin, Adams, Washington, Jefferson, and John Marshall. Like Trumbull, I have selected a few representative moments ranging from Boston in 1720 to Washington in 1803, occasions when these men created special public identities and may have measured themselves against other models or ideals. I have traced congruences between these early Americans and some older or alien cultural heroes and have examined each founder's words and deeds in order to distinguish his uniqueness in a passing instant of self-definition.

In his old age John Adams grew irritable about his small share of fame. He sometimes complained that Washington, Jefferson, and others had been blessed with a knack for making dramatic gestures, what he called *coups de théâtre*. Washington's famous resignations and farewells, Jefferson's penning of the declaration—what were these but shrewdly stage-

8. Illustrations and Lavater's commentaries are reproduced in a good general introduction to silhouettes, R. L. Mégroz, *Profile Art through the Ages* (London: Art Trade Press, 1948), pp. 61–69, 127–31.

9. See E. Neville Jackson, *The History of Silhouettes* (London: Connoisseur, 1911), pp. 8–9, and *Silhouette: Notes and Dictionary* (London: Methuen, 1938), p. 47; and Alice Van Leer Carrick, *Shades of Our Ancestors* (Boston: Little, Brown, 1928), pp. 125–32.

managed events meant for the history books?[10] Such dramatic gestures, however, were not only "masks and veils and cloaks," which Adams charged were dazzling and blinding the common people and posterity alike. Nor were they simple bids for personal glory. They also compressed deeply held beliefs into brief and memorable images—making them vivid and effective in common American life. To be fully understood, they should be examined anew along with the extensive, explicit, and sometimes impassioned writings these men left to posterity. Like Trumbull's paintings, there was more to these gestures than meets the eye.

Where words coincide with effective gestures, a skilled rhetorician is at work. These rhetorical identities arose from the stress of conflict: young Franklin asserting a new competence and outwitting his masters; Adams debating a persuasive Loyalist on the eve of the Revolution; Washington celebrating liberty in the midst of war and composing a farewell meant to sting as well as to soothe; Jefferson confronting Hamilton; Marshall confronting Jefferson. Here each of the founders meets a strong adversary and conveys an ideal truth in the face of the other's power. Under these pressures each recalls a well-known model from the past. But in the New World, addressing a revolutionary generation, he also steps forward to project an American silhouette.

10. John Adams to Benjamin Rush, September 30, 1805, July 25, 1808, and June 21, 1811, in John A. Schutz and Douglass Adair, eds., *The Spur of Fame: Dialogues of John Adams and Benjamin Rush, 1805–1813* (San Marino, Calif.: Huntington Library, 1966), pp. 43, 113, 181.

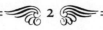

2

The Spectator's Apprentice

Craftsman, entrepreneur, scientist, inventor, public benefactor, diplomat, revolutionary, moralist, and wit—Benjamin Franklin is not easy to comprehend. One feels pride in the man and even shares his obvious delight in being intelligent, hardworking, plain, playful, and successful. But it is difficult to examine his life without becoming baffled. Along with successes at every turn—some even seeming to grow out of his famous "errata," or moral lapses—his life holds secrets and snarls of contradiction. The great exponent of thrift also relished his extravagant comforts. The sturdy Philadelphia householder enjoyed being the man of another family for long years in England and the darling of the ladies in Paris. Dr. Franklin the celebrated scientist and founder of the University of Pennsylvania sometimes boasted of the formal education he lacked. He was proud to stand before kings, yet just as proud to do without them. He was honorable yet cunning, pious but irreverent, generous but calculating, ambitious to reach heaven but crafty enough to try first with a paper kite.

Most maddening of all, he managed to make his unique successes look simple. Read carefully, his life story is a series of missteps as much as successes. He ran away from home and was flattered into a fool's errand to England; rescued by a patron who suddenly died, he imprudently married a bigamist's widow (or so she hoped) and eventually found a way to buy out his ne'er-do-well business partner to make a life of his own. Chance, fortune, providence, the Almighty (Franklin is never sure what to call it) shaped his early career as much as his own effort. But Franklin the reflective narrator keeps urging another line. His *Autobiography* persistently asserts that every event carries a moral lesson—if not on the high themes of Temperance, Industry, and Frugality, then in more mundane terms of a quiet but driving opportunism. Another complexity arises, too. From one angle, Franklin seems to regard himself as unique, as the only person in the world who could have accomplished all that he did. From another, he looks back with amusement on his commonsensical solutions to simple problems. Why, anyone could have seen that flat panes of glass were better than round globes in street lamps, that streets could be kept clean at trifling expense, that porridge made a better breakfast than beer. But the two views in tandem result in a low assessment of most other human beings. If anyone could have done all these things, and only Franklin did them, then mustn't his fellows have been lazy and dull? The indictment still holds. Franklin attained riches, fame, and wisdom; given the benefit of his example, everyone should succeed. This reproach has been drummed into generations of Americans bent over Franklin's pages.

A shining example of these complexities is Franklin's famous description of his first arrival in Philadelphia. From the start the narrator urges the reader to see more than meets the eye. He begins:

> I have been the more particular in this Description of my Journey and shall be so of my first Entry into that City, that you may in your Mind compare such unlikely Beginnings with the Figure I have since made there. I was in my Working Dress, my best Cloaths being to come round by Sea. I was dirty from my Journey; my Pockets were stuff'd out with Shirts and Stockings; I knew no Soul, nor where to look for Lodging. I was fatigu'd with Travelling, Rowing and Want of Rest. I was very hungry, and my whole Stock of Cash consisted of a Dutch Dollar and about a Shilling in Copper. The latter I gave the People of the Boat for my Passage, who at first refus'd it on Account of my Rowing; but I insisted on their taking it, a Man being sometimes

more generous when he has but a little Money than when he has plenty, perhaps thro' Fear of being thought to have but little.[1]

This first paragraph seems to be a straight description of how "unlikely" the new figure was in this strange setting. But the last sentence makes us pause. Why is someone so poor so generous? The sentence itself seems to give an answer, but it is ambiguous. In one reading, it is a bit of homely psychology, something out of Poor Richard. In another, it may be a flash of self-revelation from an old man who still identifies with this young adventurer and still wonders at the difference between being poor and being rich.

The next paragraph is even more ambiguous:

Then I walk'd up the Street, gazing about, till near the Market House I met a Boy with Bread. I had made many a Meal on Bread, and inquiring where he got it, I went immediately to the Baker's he directed me to in second Street; and ask'd for Bisket, intending such as we had in Boston, but they it seems were not made in Philadelphia, then I ask'd for a threepenny Loaf, and was told they had none such: so not considering or knowing the Difference of Money and the greater Cheapness nor the Names of his Bread, I bad him give me three penny worth of any sort. He gave me accordingly three great Puffy Rolls. I was surpriz'd at the Quantity, but took it, and having no room in my Pockets, walk'd off, with a Roll under each Arm, and eating the other. Thus I went up Market Street as far as fourth Street, passing by the Door of Mr. Read, my future Wife's Father, when she standing at the Door saw me, and thought I made as I certainly did a most awkward ridiculous Appearance. Then I turn'd and went down Chestnut Street and part of Walnut Street, eating my Roll all the Way, and coming round found my self again at Market Street Wharff, near the Boat I came in, to which I went for a Draught of the River Water, and being fill'd with one of my Rolls, gave the other two to a Woman and her Child that came down the River in the Boat with us and were waiting to go farther. Thus refresh'd I walk'd again up the

1. *The Autobiography of Benjamin Franklin*, ed. Leonard W. Labaree, Ralph L. Ketcham, Helen C. Boatfield, and Helene H. Fineman (New Haven: Yale University Press, 1964), p. 75; hereafter cited in the text as *ABF*.

Street, which by this time had many clean dress'd People in it who were all walking the same Way; I join'd them, and thereby was led into the great Meeting House of the Quakers near the Market. I sat down among them, and after looking round a while and hearing nothing said, being very drowzy thro' Labour and want of Rest the preceding Night, I fell fast asleep, and continu'd so till the Meeting broke up, when one was kind enough to rouse me. This was therefore the first House I was in or slept in, in Philadelphia. (*ABF,* pp. 75–76)

This is an evident success story. By the end of the paragraph, the newcomer has found all the necessities of life—food, shelter, a first glimpse of a helpmate, even a secure and welcoming place where all the "clean dress'd People" go. But the paragraph requires further analysis. This boy—wandering in the streets poor and slightly confused—nevertheless feels rich enough to give away two of his rolls and competent to survive on what little he has. He makes "a most awkward ridiculous Appearance," but he does so in the eyes of someone who will always remember and love him. He is so exhausted he falls asleep in church. But it is in a meeting of silent Quakers, where any stranger might be bored and benumbed. We may start by laughing *at* this silly runaway, but we grow to laugh *with* him. For this is Ben Franklin who upon his arrival has found his way to the center of town—his first step toward becoming a preeminent citizen of Philadelphia, America, and the world.

To an eighteenth-century reader this passage must have seemed familiar. It is another version of Robinson Crusoe struggling ashore and beginning to construct a prosperous life out of unlikely materials. Better yet, it is Gulliver—on a Voyage to the Land of the Quakers—wide-eyed and disadvantaged, yet destined to become, in time, the shrewd counselor and then the wise survivor of petty governors and kings. To us the story is more familiar as the fable of the self-made man, the well-worn American tale of the pioneer for whom the past is lost and the present threatening, but the future is an unlimited golden realm to be achieved through sweat and daring. For Franklin's story, however, none of these patterns is quite right. The narrator is too playful, too sophisticated, too deep to be caught in any formula. The life itself was as full of quirks as of energy, and the retelling is in prose that is hardly simple even on the surface.

There is evidence, however, that helps explain Franklin's complexity. In the end we have to admit we know only a little of how anyone achieves complexity. But enough is preserved from Franklin's youth to show that he had great advantages. The years before he arrived in Philadelphia were not lost, either in his development or in the public record. In those years he had already achieved many of the things for which he later became famous. He had learned his trade as a printer. He had seen how scientific experiments could produce great public benefits. He had mastered some complicated and dangerous political maneuvering, singlehandedly articulating the mood of an entire city. And he had practiced and perfected a straightforward but sinuous style of prosewriting, which he copied from contemporary European masters.

In Boston in 1722 young Franklin was involved in a crisis between an outworn but tenacious old order and a new kind of power emerging in his brother's print shop. A smallpox epidemic had broken out in 1721, and the Puritan clergy, led by Cotton Mather, had supported a limited experiment with inoculation. Franklin's brother James started a newspaper, the *New-England Courant,* and published expert medical opinion against the practice. He thus opened a means of expression for long-suppressed resentments against the Puritan ministers. The quarrel went on for months, outlasting the epidemic, and in the end no one won. On the one hand, the *Courant* ceased to publish in 1726 and James Franklin fled to Rhode Island, where he died in 1735. On the other, the clergy's authority was diminished. The ministers had been publicly challenged, questioned, and caught in a paradox of their own making: they were urging a strange new science in the face of a scourge from God. For young Benjamin, however, the controversy opened a new way to bring his talents before the public. And he had prepared himself thoroughly for the opportunity. He was ready to surprise Boston, his brother, and Cotton Mather, too, with some novel strategies of London journalism.

Franklin had served four years as his brother's apprentice when the epidemic broke out. As the *Autobiography* explains, he trained as a printer with his brother because it was beyond his father's means to send him to Harvard; since no other trade interested him, he had threatened to run away to sea. But the printer's trade held some appeal for him. He did not remember a time when he could not read, the shop offered a wealth of published learning, and he found the money and time to buy and pore over other books. In return, the books changed him. One led him to vegetarianism; another taught him the Socratic method of disputation; yet another helped him master the arithmetic he had failed at school. But the book he remembered best was a collection of essays: "About this time I met with an odd Volume of the Spectator. It was the third. I had never before seen any of them. I bought it, read it over and over, and was much delighted with it. I thought the Writing excellent and wish'd if possible to imitate it" (*ABF*, pp. 61–62).

Franklin described how he was at pains to imitate these writings. He took notes on issues of the *Spectator,* sentence by sentence, and tried to rewrite the essays. Later, "I took some of the Tales and turn'd them into Verse: And after a time, when I had pretty well forgotten the Prose, turn'd them back again. I also sometimes jumbled my Collections of Hints into Confusion, and after some Weeks, endeavour'd to reduce them into the best Order before I began to form the full Sentences and compleat the Paper. This was to teach me Method in the Arrangement of Thoughts." Franklin not only overcame his faults but also discovered sparks of talent in his revisions, which "encouraged me to think I might possibly in time come to be a tolerable English Writer, of which I was extremely ambitious" (*ABF,* p. 62).

His study of Addison and Steele had lasting effects. The *Courant* papers Franklin wrote in 1722–23 and the early Busy Body papers of 1729 are clearly modeled on features of the *Tatler, Spectator,* and *Guardian.* Selections from the *Spectator* and *Guardian* are quoted in late numbers of the Silence Dogood series. When he published the *Pennsylvania Gazette* (1729–47), Franklin "frequently reprinted in it Extracts from the Spectator" (*ABF,* p. 165). And when he drew up his *Proposals relating to the Education of Youth in Pennsylvania* (1749), he listed Addison as a model stylist and prescribed a method of learning composition much like his own: abstracting and later rewriting passages of exemplary prose.

So far, we have an edifying case of successful self-education. But we can also see something that Franklin, even in his *Autobiography,* did not: that his hours of practice with the *Spectator* matched the experience of many other eighteenth-century readers. As far away as Sumatra readers were modeling their styles upon its pages. Voltaire used it to improve his

English in 1726. In his early journals Boswell often resolved to reform himself and be more like Addison or wrote of entertaining himself by viewing London scenes he had read about in the *Spectator*. Two authorities on style also recommended the journal. Hugh Blair asked his students to imitate *Spectator* papers and analyzed some of them himself. And Dr. Johnson concluded his life of Addison with the famous pronouncement: "Whoever wishes to attain an English style, familiar but not coarse, and elegant but not ostentatious, must give his days and nights to the volumes of Addison."[2]

These writers echoed Addison and Steele themselves, who frequently boasted that their brief but polished essays were models for young men wanting to acquire a proper style in prose, manners, and life itself. In number 428 of the *Spectator,* Steele wrote that the journal was as suitable to the "Youth in his Apprenticeship" as to "Men of Literature." The design of appealing to all sorts of readers was apparent from the first. The famous opening paragraph of number 10 emphasized the point that daily essays would be short and frequent enough to serve as mental setting-up exercises. "Since I have raised to my self so great an Audience," Mr. Spectator vowed, "I shall spare no Pains to make their Instruction agreeable, and their Diversion useful. . . . And to the end that their Virtue and Discretion may not be short transient intermitting Starts of Thought, I have resolved to refresh their Memories from Day to Day, till I have recovered them out of that desperate State of Vice and Folly into which the Age is fallen." In fact, Addison sought to provide his readers with a course of moral lectures every Saturday as well as serious discussions of wit, poetry, and manners. It was not only Franklin's genius, then, that made the *Spectator* useful to him. The journal itself was meant to provide pleasant models for those who lacked a library or formal instruction.

The success of the *Tatler* and *Spectator* also made them invaluable to any bright printer's apprentice. They were not merely newspapers but an innovation in the new world of journalism. Instead of offering only sober news, they discoursed on hundreds of topics of interest to general readers, both men and women. In the years between 1709 and 1712 they sold as fast as the press could produce them—a lesson not lost on Franklin's

2. *The Spectator,* ed. Donald F. Bond, 5 vols. (Oxford: Clarendon Press, 1965), 1:lxxxvi–lxxxvii, xcix-c. All quotations from the *Spectator* hereafter are from this edition.

brother James. He had served his apprenticeship in London, returning to Boston in 1717 and briefly printing the *Boston Gazette* for the local postmaster in 1719–20. But when he came to launch his own *Courant,* he produced a sheet of witty social commentary in imitation of the first issue of the *Spectator.* "I have observed," Addison had begun, "that a Reader seldom peruses a Book with Pleasure 'till he knows whether the Writer of it be a black or a fair Man, of a mild or cholerick Disposition, Married or a Batchelor, with other Particulars of the like nature, that conduce very much to the right Understanding of an Author." He introduced Mr. Spectator as a figure who would remain neutral in all public disputes, and he invited contributions from London's readers. Observe the opening of the first *Courant:* "It's an hard Case, that a Man can't appear in Print now a Days, unless he'll undergo the Mortification of Answering to ten thousand senseless and Impertinent Questions like these, *Pray Sir, from whence came you? And what Age may you be of, may I be so bold? Was you bred at Colledge, Sir?*" The second issue opened with a further notice: "At the desire of several Gentlemen in Town, this Paper is to be published weekly. The Publisher earnestly desires his Friends may favour him from time to time, with some short Piece, *Serious; Sarcastick, Ludicrous,* or otherways amusing; or sometimes *professedly Dull,* (to accomodate some of his acquaintance) that this *Courant* may be of the more universal Use."[3] The design and language are more rustic, but the resemblances to the *Spectator* are plain. Thus Ben Franklin sharpened his skills by learning both from his brother and collaborators and from the pages of the *Spectator.* The apprentice and his immediate masters were trying to imitate the same influential model.

Meanwhile Addison's work was having some influence in other parts of Boston. Here too it excited admiration and imitation—but with a difference. At Harvard a manuscript journal was circulating with a title—the *Telltale*—that recalled the *Tatler* and features that resembled pieces in the *Spectator.*[4] And in his diary for August 4, 1713, Cotton Mather wrote,

3. *New-England Courant,* August 7 and 14, 1721, quoted from microform copies of the file kept by Benjamin Franklin and preserved in the British Museum and (in photocopy) at the Massachusetts Historical Society. For a description of this file, see Worthington C. Ford, "Franklin's New England Courant," Massachusetts Historical Society, *Proceedings* 57 (1923–24): 336–53. In the originals, these notices were printed in italics, with stressed words in Roman.

4. Samuel Eliot Morison, *Three Centuries of Harvard, 1636–1936* (Cambridge, Mass.: Harvard University Press, 1936), pp. 60–63.

"Perhaps, by sending some agreeable Things, to the Author of, *The Spectator,* and, *The Guardian,* there may be brought forward some Services to the best Interests in the Nation."[5]

Cotton Mather was considerably older than Franklin and his brother. At the time of the smallpox crisis, he was nearly sixty, with a full and varied career behind him and a bibliography to match. As recent biographers have stressed, he saw himself as the personification of New England learning and piety. He was eager to absorb new ideas and to pass them on to a people who had long respected the wisdom of his forebears.[6] It is not surprising, then, that the *Spectator* had caught his eye. The author of *Bonafacius* (or as Franklin called it, "Essays to do Good") would have seen in its pages projects for social reforms and reports of their success. As a Fellow of the Royal Society, he would have been interested in the journal's accounts of scientific discoveries and their religious applications. As the compiler of New England history, he might well have envied the wide fame of Mr. Spectator's essays and been eager to correct the impression that only the Indian chiefs who visited Queen Anne were topics of interest from the New World. And Mather must also have seen in the sudden and lasting influence of the *Spectator* an alternative to his own method of addressing his fellowmen.

Like most Puritan clergymen, Mather faced his people directly. As his father's colleague in Boston's North Church, he visited, taught, exhorted, and preached to his congregation; he disputed and conferred with his fellow ministers in New England; and he advised and maneuvered at several levels of colonial government. At the same time he wrote and published (often in London) scores of tracts and books to impress his readers with the force of abstract reasoning and wide learning. Like many another seventeenth-century divine—and like his father and grandfathers before him—he was concerned that both his congregation and the world at large should hear the truths he proclaimed. But Cotton Mather's world was different from the great religious realm of his predecessors; though he wrote and published

5. *The Diary of Cotton Mather, 1704–1724,* Massachusetts Historical Society, *Collections,* 7th ser., 8 (1912): 227; subsequent quotations are from this edition and are cited in the text by date.

6. This conception of Mather has been fully explored and contrasted to Franklin's individualistic, calculating character in Mitchell Robert Breitweiser, *Cotton Mather and Benjamin Franklin: The Price of Representative Personality* (New York: Cambridge University Press, 1985).

more than any of them, the world was changing and cared less now about the spiritual wonders offered by Puritan New England.

The *Spectator,* in contrast, had an advantage: Mr. Spectator and his fellow clubmen were not actual persons, yet they dispensed moral advice in the journal's daily issues and circulated readers' letters attesting to their own good works. A fictitious spokesman like Mr. Spectator could seem more authoritative than any mere mortal. Who could challenge his assertions of familiarity with learned books and his knowledge of curiosities from every age and region of the world? Like Isaac Bickerstaff of the *Tatler,* he set himself up as a *censor morum* and presided over his public as though it were one vast assenting congregation. Thus the Mathers, who had toiled through generations to maintain authority over their community, were confronted by a new age of communication. Journals like the *Spectator* assumed immediate authority and sustained it with whatever success they enjoyed from week to week. Mather had reason to see this new power of the press as a blessing or a curse, depending on how it was used. With the outbreak of smallpox in Boston, he had occasion to see it both ways at once.

Two successive entries in his diary display this ambivalence. The first, dated August 24, 1721, was written shortly after the *Courant* began to appear. The voice is that of Cotton Mather, the vehemently self-righteous Puritan:

> This Town is become almost an Hell upon Earth, a City full of Lies, and Murders, and Blasphemies, as far as Wishes and Speeches can render it so; Satan seems to take a strange Possession of it, in the epidemic Rage, against that notable and powerful and successful way of saving the lives of People from the Dangers of the *Small-Pox.* What can I do on this Occasion, to gett the miserable Town dispossessed of the evil Spirit, which has taken such an horrible Possession of it? What besides Prayer with Fasting, for it?

This is the Matherean mind that saw Satan guiding his adversaries, that had seen witches at Salem, that pronounced the *Courant* the product of an illegal Hell-Fire Club, that dared to surmise that God might strike James Franklin dead for his impieties. But within a day Mather penned another entry that answered his last question with a voice from a later century:

I will assist my Physician, in giving to the Public, some Accounts about releeving the *Small-Pox* in the way of *Transplantation;* which may be of great Consequence!

Undaunted by the press, he would use it himself and win over the public by careful accounts of what he and Zabdiel Boylston together could achieve in preventive medicine.

Mather's part in the smallpox controversy remains difficult to assess. He has been seen even recently as a dabbler in strange arts who overreached his authority as a clergyman by urging a new practice on a community frantic with fear of the scourge. Dr. William Douglass at the time charged that inoculation was untried and dangerous, especially since inoculated patients might spread the disease. And Douglass, who often wrote for the *Courant,* carried the authority of being the one Boston physician with an earned medical degree. According to this view, Mather happened upon inoculation by chance and avoided disaster only by sheer luck. Even so, the limits of his powers as a community leader and as a covenant theologian were exposed. According to another view, however, Mather's papers reveal him as a patient, cautious, courageous pioneer in modern medicine. He had studied medical literature and scientific lore for many years. He learned of inoculation from his black slave before he read of it in the *Philosophical Transactions,* and he wrote to the Royal Society seeking advice on the practice as early as 1716. When the disease broke out, he communicated what he knew and arranged a meeting of Boston physicians to urge them to consider inoculation. Only Boylston agreed to the experiment, but Mather supported him through his writings. He inoculated members of his own family and then became anguished when his son Samuel developed the disease as a result. In November someone threw a bomb into his house, along with a note protesting the new practice. Yet he persevered and he helped save lives, just as Charles Maitland and Lady Mary Wortley Montagu were doing at about the same time in England.[7] Unfortu-

7. The first view is fully treated in Perry Miller, *The New England Mind: From Colony to Province* (Cambridge, Mass.: Harvard University Press, 1953), pp. 345–66, and repeated in Robert Middlekauff, *The Mathers: Three Generations of Puritan Intellectuals, 1596–1728* (New York: Oxford University Press, 1971), p. 356. The second view is presented in George Lyman Kittredge, "Some Lost Works of Cotton Mather," Massachusetts Historical Society, *Proceedings* 45 (1911–12): 418–79, and Otho T. Beall, Jr., and Richard H. Shryock, *Cotton Mather: First Significant Figure in American Medicine* (Baltimore: Johns Hopkins Press, 1954). Kenneth Silverman, *The Life and Times of Cotton Mather* (New York:

nately, however, neither an advanced modern researcher nor an impulsive zealot can be distilled pure from Mather's life in these months. The outbreak of smallpox greatly upset public life in Boston, then a town of about eleven thousand, and an eruption of provocative challenges from the *Courant* and other quarters drove Mather into excess. The documents he left display credulity, learning, wilfulness, piety, and intellectual penetration all tangled beyond unraveling.

In any case, Mather soon found himself confronting the worst effects of Addisonian irony. And Franklin's *Autobiography* suggests that events unfolded to give the young apprentice an invigorating review of the lessons he had been learning on his own. Franklin must have read the *Spectator* and practiced his imitations well before the smallpox crisis because he claims he had not seen the work before he bought the odd volume that got him started. Yet when the *Courant* began, it obviously copied that London journal. Franklin's exercise book suddenly became his brother's chief weapon. Moreover, the *Courant* was aimed directly at Cotton Mather, the most learned man in Boston, and it successfully challenged him on his own terms. Franklin himself was intimately involved: "After having work'd in composing the Types and printing off the Sheets I was employ'd to carry the Papers thro' the Streets to the Customers" (*ABF*, p. 67). Thus while Mather watched over his experiment in inoculation, the Franklins were countering with a daring experiment of their own. The first issue of the *Courant* carried verses against men

> Who like faithful Shepherds take care of their *Flocks,*
> By teaching and practising what's Orthodox,
> Pray hard against *Sickness,* yet preach up the *POX!*

The early issues featured articles against inoculation, and from week to week the *Courant* continued to beard Mather directly. The issue for December 4 reported that in November the doctor met James Franklin on the street and rebuked him for vilifying the ministers. Franklin defended

---

Harper & Row, 1984) thoroughly reviews Mather's work in this period (pp. 336–63) and concludes that he was enlightened, heroic, and caring despite his personal vehemence in the midst of controversy. Breitweiser (pp. 117–32) argues that inoculation, rightly understood, was an intrinsic concern in Mather's career; he spent his life trying to preserve the body of his community against the onslaught of evil.

himself, but he also showed a wry detachment by printing Mather's version of the encounter in the same paper.

To be sure, the Mathers responded in kind. Thomas Walter, Mather's nephew, wrote a broadside, *Little-Compton Scourge: or, the Anti-Courant* (also printed by Franklin), which attempted to counter wit with wit. On August 18 Mather wrote in his diary, "I may propose some agreeable Passages, to be inserted in the *News-Letters*, which have a Notable Tendency to correct and restrain the Epidemical Follies of the Town." The strong letter against the *Courant* in the *News-Letter* of August 28 may well be his. In January, his father, Increase Mather, wrote a formal "Advice to the Public" in the *Gazette* against the *Courant*. And Samuel Mather, Cotton's son and Benjamin Franklin's contemporary, was still writing against it under the name "John Harvard" several weeks later.[8]

The smallpox crisis thus precipitated a longer contest between clergy and press. By winter the epidemic began to wane, but the fever in the newspapers continued. Benjamin Franklin must have watched this struggle with mixed feelings. He had long since given up churchgoing to gain time for secular reading, but he had read some of Mather's works with admiration. Mather's *Essays to Do Good*, he said later, "perhaps gave me a Turn of Thinking that had an Influence on some of the principal future Events of my Life" (*ABF*, p. 58). Now the lively controversy between the *Courant* and the ministers excited his own desire to write. His brother "had some ingenious Men among his Friends who amus'd themselves by writing little Pieces for this Paper, which gain'd it Credit, and made it more in Demand; and these Gentlemen often visited us. Hearing their Conversations, and their Accounts of the Approbation their Papers were receiv'd with, I was excited to try my Hand among them" (*ABF*, p. 67). The result, after months of consideration, was a series of fourteen papers from "Silence Dogood," which ran in the *Courant* from April to October 1722.

These admittedly imitative papers derived from many sources. Most of them reflected on local controversies or on earlier discussions in the *Courant*.[9] And their debt to the *Spectator* has been discussed so often there is no need to trace the analogies in every issue. What we can now appreciate

8. *Boston Gazette*, January 29 and 15, 1721–22, and May 28, 1722.
9. George F. Horner, "Franklin's *Dogood Papers* Re-examined," *Studies in Philology* 37 (1940): 501–32.

is the way Franklin balanced his British models and Bostonian influences and so produced a more polished set of writings than anyone else could have written for this public.

He began with a great advantage, by making up a fictitious authorial identity and keeping himself strictly out of sight. Part of James Franklin's problem in attempting *Spectator*-like wit had been that he was personally too conspicuous. There was no disguising that a quarrel was going on between the *Courant*'s editor and the Mathers. This problem was endemic in early journalism. It had plagued Defoe in the *Review* (1704–13) and John Tutchin in the *Observator* (1702–07).[10] But the *Tatler* and the *Spectator* had kept their authors obscured until Steele signed their final numbers; Addison was never mentioned by name. Readers, playing along with a patently fictitious editor, used him as the object of their praise or irritation. Young Ben Franklin followed the same procedure: "But being still a Boy, and suspecting that my Brother would object to printing any Thing of mine in his Paper if he knew it to be mine, I contriv'd to disguise my Hand, and writing an anonymous Paper I put it in at Night under the Door of the Printing House." This first Dogood paper was found, read, and approved by the *Courant* staff and was followed by others in a regular series, all conveyed to the paper in the same way. "I kept my Secret till my small Fund of Sense for such Performances was pretty well exhausted, and then I discovered it" (*ABF,* pp. 67–68). James Franklin had published other contributions under absurd pseudonyms—"Ichabod Henroost" or "Fanny Mournful"—but this was the first series to be sustained under an assumed identity. And the apprentice remained comfortably hidden even from his brother the editor, free to shape this identity with the play of an alert imagination.

To begin his sketch, Franklin borrowed and combined many features that would tease contemporary readers. Each suggests a definite point of view or firmness of character at first, yet quickly dissolves into the generally agreeable and appealing figure of a composite fiction. What are we to make of the fact that these letters were attributed to a woman, the widow of a country minister, with the name Silence Dogood? Some of them seem to comment on public affairs or on Franklin's own life. He had been

10. L. S. Horsley, "Rogues or Honest Gentlemen: The Public Characters of Queen Anne Journalists," *Texas Studies in Literature and Language* 18 (1976): 198–228.

arguing with a friend that women could study and learn as well as men. He was addressing a town where widows, from smallpox and other causes, were numerous. The mention of ministers and Dogood might bring the Mathers to mind. Yet all these features conform to the conventions of current essay periodicals. Mr. Spectator was conspicuous for his taciturnity. Both he and Bickerstaff made a point of addressing their educable female readers. And along with many other journalists they set out to reform their readers by drawing on their own learning and, on occasion, on the counsel of clergymen. As the widow tells her history in the first two papers, she reveals a character that is true to this form. She has had varied experiences and access to books—enough to make her authoritative on a wide range of subjects. But she is also ingratiating; she is obscure and humble and a little absurd—as when she narrates how her father was killed the day she was born, carried away by joy and salty waves.

As we saw earlier, the *Courant* began by imitating the line in the first issue of the *Spectator* about whether the editor was "a black or a fair Man, of a mild or cholerick Disposition, Married or a Batchelor." Silence Dogood begins with a passage even closer to the original:

And since it is observed, that the Generality of People, now a days, are unwilling either to commend or dispraise what they read, until they are in some measure informed who or what the Author of it is, whether he be *poor* or *rich, old* or *young,* a *Schollar* or a *Leather Apron Man,* &c. and give their Opinion of the Performance, according to the knowledge with they have of the Author's Circumstances, it may not be amiss to begin with a short Account of my past Life and present Condition, that the Reader may not be at a Loss to judge whether or no my Lucubrations are worth his reading.[11]

The passage in the *Spectator* was carefully designed to let readers know they were not dealing with a real editor's introduction. Mr. Spectator finally did *not* reveal whether he was black or fair, mild or choleric; instead he went on to show that he would have something worth reading for all types of subscribers. Read carefully, his opening remarks tell the reader to hold the paper at arm's length and look beyond impertinent questions

11. *The Papers of Benjamin Franklin,* ed. Leonard W. Labaree et al. (New Haven: Yale University Press, 1959-), 1:9; hereafter cited in the text as *Papers.*

about the author. This Dogood passage works in the same way. The word *lucubrations* at the end signals that this contributor knows what he is about; the *Tatler*s were called lucubrations and were republished as *The Lucubrations of Isaac Bickerstaff, Esq.* This writer too imputes curiosity about an author to "the Generality of People" and agrees to satisfy it only as a sop to gross taste. And he sets up alternatives that turn out to be meaningless. We never know whether Silence Dogood is poor or rich, old or young. The point about whether the author is a scholar or a leather-apron man has more bite. The *Courant* has been attacked as the work of mere leather-apron men, whereas the Mathers and their allies were Harvard scholars. But it is wrong to conclude that Franklin is here taking upon himself a symbolic role, or fashioning a vehicle for his own apprentice view of society, or dividing Boston into camps opposed over the worth of the *Courant*.[12] The phrase fits into a paragraph that laughs away these contrasts. The widow Silence Dogood is clearly neither scholar nor man. As for Franklin, it is a nice question where he was not seeing himself here, with amusement, as a leather-apron scholar triumphing under the noses of both the Mathers and his brother. What is clear is that this invisible author is opening a delightful game of Addisonian evasion.

The same elusiveness plays through the other papers in the series. In one Mrs. Dogood presents Defoe's serious proposal for insuring wives against widowhood—a Dogood project, perfectly in character. But in the next she pokes fun at this scheme when a poor spinster asks for similar benefits. In numbers 8 and 9 Franklin published what he later called satiric "rubs" against the local rulers. But unlike the direct taunting that put his brother in jail at this time, these papers waver over whether there exist any local problems of free speech or hypocrisy, and Mrs. Dogood is content to stand aside and quote from the *London Journal.* When she writes a critical dream allegory of Harvard in number 4, she frames the satire in a conversation with her "reverend boarder" about sending her own son there. And in the next issue she considers whether she ought to concentrate on the follies of her own sex.

The paper on drunkenness, number 12, shows how the author could shift ground from paragraph to paragraph, to tease readers out of thinking too

12. Miller, pp. 361–62; Carl Van Doren, *Benjamin Franklin* (New York: Viking, 1938), pp. 21–22; Horner, p. 513.

seriously or moralistically. The paper opens with the promise of an object lesson. "A true and natural Representation of any Enormity, is often the best Argument against it and Means of removing it, when the most severe Reprehensions alone, are found ineffectual." But in the third paragraph we soon find that drinking is not entirely an "enormity": "much Study and Experience, and a little Liquor, are of absolute Necessity for some Tempers, in order to make them accomplish'd Orators." Then Mrs. Dogood laughs at her sex for becoming eloquent because of passion instead of liquor. She goes on to castigate immoderate drinkers—because they become either outrageously profane or unnaturally religious: "Some shrink in the Wetting, and others swell." The paper concludes with a list of slang terms for drunkenness: "In short, every Day produces some new Word or Phrase which might be added to the Vocabulary of the *Tiplers:* But I have chose to mention these few, because if at any Time a Man of Sobriety and Temperance happens to *cut himself confoundedly,* or is *almost froze,* or *feavourish,* or accidentally *sees the Sun,* &c. he may escape the Imputation of being *drunk,* when his Misfortune comes to be related" (*Papers,* 1:41). We end with laughter, and to ask whether this paper castigates or celebrates drunkenness is to miss the point.

The entire series is a far cry from pulpit moralism and stands just as far from the *Courant*'s sallies against the Mathers. It was an effective adaptation of Addisonian art to American circumstances and one of the most perceptive sequels to the *Spectator* to have been produced anywhere.

During the run of this series, however, the career of the *Courant* was approaching its climax. On May 15, when the government prohibited Boylston from performing further inoculations, the campaign was won. But already James had been imprisoned for his offensive journalism and worse was to come. Poor James Franklin! Coping with forces civil, medical, and ecclesiastical was work enough for a pioneer of freedom of the press. But at the same time the man had to witness his brother's emergence as a celebrity and rival under his own roof. The *Autobiography* leaves no doubt that the young Benjamin Franklin could be dogged as an adversary and ostentatious in triumph. When he finally revealed that it was his hand behind the Dogood papers, it gave him status in the eyes of the *Courant* group and led to more blows between master and apprentice.

In a few months, however, the struggle between them was reversed.

James had continued to taunt the authorities, and in January 1723 he was ordered to submit to prior censorship or give up publishing any newspaper. When he defied this command, he was ordered arrested for contempt. A consultation among the *Courant* authors resulted in a new scheme. The paper would be brought out under Benjamin Franklin's name. "And to avoid the Censure of the Assembly that might fall on him [James], as still printing it by his Apprentice, the Contrivance was, that my old Indenture should be return'd to me with a full Discharge on the Back of it, to be shown on Occasion; but to secure him the Benefit of my Service I was to sign new Indentures for the Remainer of the Term, which were to be kept private" (*ABF*, pp. 69–70). The new arrangement went into effect on February 11, and the struggle between James and Benjamin became public. Who was now whose brother's keeper? In September Benjamin resolved the situation by moving to Philadelphia. The apprenticeship was over, and the *Courant* passed from success to a long decline.

But at the crucial moment, when the editorship shifted in the *Courant* of February 11, 1723, Benjamin Franklin presented himself once more as a thoroughgoing Addisonian. After writing some paragraphs disdaining public rancor and promising to turn instead to genteel entertainments and "a grateful Interspersion of more serious Morals," Franklin projected a new editorial figure. "As for the Author, that is the next Question. But tho' we profess our selves ready to oblige the ingenious and courteous Reader with most Sorts of Intelligence, yet here we beg a Reserve." Instead of giving real identities, the *Courant* would furnish only that familiar compound ghost, a new mock-editor standing in for an anonymous group of collaborators.

> The Society had design'd to present the Publick with his Effigies, but that the Limner, to whom he was presented for a Draught of his Countenance, descryed (and this he is ready to offer upon Oath) Nineteen Features in his Face, more than ever he beheld in any Humane Visage before; which so raised the Price of his Picture, that our Master himself forbid the Extravagance of coming up to it. And then besides, the Limner objected a Schism in his Face, which splits from his Forehead in a strait Line down to his Chin, in such sort, that Mr. Painter protests it is a double Face, and he'll have *Four Pounds* for the Pourtraiture. However,

tho' this double Face has spoilt us of a pretty Picture, yet we all rejoiced to see old Janus in our Company.

There is no Man in Boston better qualified than old Janus for a *Couranteer,* or if you please, an *Observator,* being a Man of such remarkable *Opticks,* as to look two ways at once. (*Papers,* 1:49–50)

Here is yet another neat but complex joke. Janus is the double face of James and Benjamin, looking back on the turbulent months of the *Courant* and forward to new prospects. The second paragraph also acknowledges that he is an optic creation, an observator, which is but another word for spectator. And a man of such optics as to look two ways at once—that is a good formula for the joco-serious, light-but-penetrating, knowing-but-unknown being that Franklin had found in Addison's pages and mastered in his own.

Franklin's education certainly did not end when he left home. But his early years gave him unique advantages for the century to come. He learned not only printing in his brother's shop but publishing with daring and imagination. He found not only limpid prose in his volume of the *Spectator* but also the knack of ingratiating himself with a public of common readers. Seeing all sides of the smallpox controversy, he was a front-row witness as a new science began to solve a centuries-old riddle and free common people from its terror. (Partly because of the Boston experiment, the murderous, scarring, highly contagious smallpox was met by more widespread inoculation in the eighteenth century.) For a moment Franklin stood on an equal footing with his brother and Cotton Mather in cultivating the moral tone of an entire city. Within one year he confronted both of these petty tyrants and went off to become his own man in a more cosmopolitan world.

Years later all these lessons remained fresh in his mind. In 1773 he exchanged some pamphlets with Samuel Mather, and on July 7 he wrote him a friendly letter from London. This was the son of Cotton Mather, the same young man who had been inoculated in 1721 and survived to write attacks upon the *Courant* in general and Silence Dogood in particular. Franklin seems to have forgotten these things if he ever knew them; in this letter he asks Samuel if he is Cotton's son or nephew. Yet he remembers one anecdote from his early years and he records it at length:

But Cotton I remember in the Vigour of his Preaching and Useful-
ness. And particularly in the Year 1723, now half a Century since, I
had reason to remember, as I still do a Piece of Advice he gave me. I
had been some time with him in his Study, where he condescended to
entertain me, a very Youth, with some pleasant and instructive Conversation. As I was taking my Leave he accompany'd me thro' a
narrow Passage at which I did not enter, and which had a Beam
across it lower than my Head. He continued Talking which occasion'd me to keep my Face partly towards him as I retired, when he
suddenly cry'd out, Stoop! Stoop! Not immediatly understanding
what he meant, I hit my Head hard against the Beam. He then added,
Let this be a Caution to you not always to hold your Head so high; Stoop,
young Man, stoop—as you go through the World—and you'll miss many
hard Thumps. This was a way of hammering instruction into one's
Head: And it was so far effectual, that I have ever since remember'd
it, tho' I have not always been able to practise it. (*Papers,* 20:287)[13]

It appears in this passage that Mather took advantage of Franklin's acci-
dent to *reinforce* a lesson he was already teaching him as they headed down
the passageway. Franklin did not understand until too late why Mather
cried "Stoop! Stoop!" The minister applied the lesson immediately, and it
"was a way of hammering Instruction into one's Head." Evidently the
conversation already concerned Franklin's conduct, his holding his head
too high. Also, the lesson remained vivid because of its date: "particularly
in the Year 1723 . . . I had reason to remember . . . a Piece of Advice."
How had Franklin found his way into Mather's study at such a time? Was
the newsboy-cum-publisher of the *Courant* delivering an issue to an avid
reader and finding himself obliged to smooth over his brother's quarrels
and hear his own position in the world anatomized? It is hard to imagine
any other reason for Mather to address this mere apprentice on such a
subject. And so we have here a last view of this whole affair: Dr. Mather
holding an office hour with a great student, and the student fifty years later
reporting it from London with the morality and wit of our most playful
public man.

13. Franklin repeated this anecdote in another letter to Samuel Mather, dated May 12, 1784, and
there dated it in 1724 when he first returned to Boston from Philadelphia. I believe this 1773 version
represents Franklin's better memory of a long-past event.

3

Novanglus

After a long eclipse, John Adams has been restored for readers in this century as both a brilliant statesman and a fascinating human character. Many of his papers have been brought to light after decades of neglect and suppression, and all his writings are now being patiently reproduced and reconstructed, supported by informed commentary, and supplemented by modern studies of his friends and close contemporaries. The result is an Adams who needs no apologies; he may be perceived not as the touchy, sturdy Bostonian who was Washington's vice president and inept successor but as a deep, learned, lucid, and often quick and entertaining man. He stands now on a par with Franklin as a canny negotiator, with Jefferson as an encyclopedic scholar, with Washington as a lover of his native soil and a deliberate but daring revolutionary. Moreover, he left thousands of pages of energetic prose, scratching observations on the important controversies, ideas, passions, and personalities of the Revolution with the sharp point of his pen.

In many ways he invites comparison with Franklin. He came from the same provincial obscurity, from the same kind of solid, modest Massachusetts family, and reached the heights of fame in both America and Europe. He stood next to Franklin on many important occasions at home and abroad (and even shared the same bed once or twice). He also rose by much the same means—applying himself diligently to his work, carefully developing a judicious public spirit, and taking conspicuous action against the injustices of provincial aristocrats. Although Adams was about thirty years younger than Franklin, we also find other common elements in their lives. He too pored over the pages of the *Spectator* and carefully copied many of them out by hand. He too first broke into print with a series of comic newspaper essays, written under a fictitious name. He too filled volumes with letters, notes, sketches, and annotations—the almost daily play (or fidgeting) of a disciplined intelligence.

But Adam's character developed through a different kind of discipline. Franklin became an eclectic young scholar and observer of men while earning his bread as a printer and publisher. Adams ripened more slowly, as a student at Harvard, a schoolmaster in Worcester, and finally a young lawyer. And when he came to the law he gave himself to it wholly. He had simple motives for choosing this profession; it promised him a good livelihood and a solid place in his society. But he came to pursue his studies and practice with a deep devotion. For Adams, law became not only a way to wealth but a way to wisdom. By mastering the law he might comprehend philosophy and politics, understand a range of sciences, and directly touch the practical concerns of his fellowmen.

In the beginning law was for him a regimen, work that he had to force himself to do; it grew to be a way of life, a complex of habits in his thinking and behavior. Such thoroughgoing discipline had three enduring results. It set the New England lawyer apart from other men, even other well-educated men. It drew a small band of these men together so that they might share their understanding of law and their reverence for British ideals of constitutional procedure. And it committed them all to sacrifice their own identities to a stable, well-understood order of society. Each of these consequences deserves some elaboration, for taken together they destined Adams and his closest contemporaries to lives that would be torn apart by the American Revolution.

Adams early realized how specialized the knowledge of law must be. When Chief Justice Sewall died in 1760 the young lawyer prepared a letter for the press, pointing out that no ordinary citizen could take up his duties. (It soon rankled Adams and others that the post went to Thomas Hutchinson, who had no formal legal training.) Adams outlined the complex sources of the law—in common law, acts of Parliament, civil law, and canon and feudal law. Only hard study from early youth could provide the knowledge "from all these sources sufficient to decide the Lives, Liberties, and fortunes of Mankind, with safety to the Peoples Liberties, as well as the Kings Prerogative, that happy Union, in which the Excellence of british Government consists, and which has often been preserved by the deep Discernment and noble spirit of english Judges." Thus he sensibly concluded that "a Man whose Youth and Spirits and Strength, have been spent, in Husbandry Merchandize, Politics, nay in science or Literature will never master so immense and involved a science."[1]

In other words, it was precisely here that the way diverged for an Adams and a Franklin. It was a young newspaper printer's business to make himself an agreeable everyman—to master the common touch or its literary equivalent, to compose a pleasing, commonplace identity to set before thousands of readers. But a young lawyer had little opportunity for popularity. He addressed himself to sophisticated judges and adversaries, readers prepared to marshal their own reserves of learning and make much of the nuances of a phrase. Adams's writings thus rely on the support of the reader's intelligence. He seems most at home among books in a study (including his own diaries), with well-tried friends and correspondents, or taking part in a regulated formal debate: a legislative assembly, a law court, or a negotiating chamber.

This does not mean that he saw himself as narrow or shut out from society. Quite the contrary. He and his fellow lawyers believed they were at the heart of society.

> Law is a sublime study, and what more sublime! what more worthy the indefatigable Labour & pursuit of a reasonable Man! than that Science by which Mankind raise themselves from the forlorn helpless State in which Nature leave's them, to the full Enjoyment of all the inestimable Blessings of Social Union, & by which, they (if you will allow the Expression) triumph over the Frailty & Imperfections of Humanity?[2]

---

1. *Diary and Autobiography of John Adams,* ed. L. H. Butterfield, 4 vols. (Cambridge, Mass.: Harvard University Press, 1961), 1:167–68; hereafter cited in the text as *D&A.*

2. Jonathan Sewall to John Adams, September 29, 1759, quoted in Carol Berkin, *Jonathan Sewall: Odyssey of an American Loyalist* (New York: Columbia University Press, 1974), p. 16.

So Jonathan Sewall wrote to Adams in 1759. Adams replied with an even more vigorous manifesto. He wrote that British law comprised all human knowledge about man, history, and eloquence. "Now to what higher object, to what greater Character, can any Mortal aspire, than to be possessed of all this Knowledge, well digested, and ready at Command, to assist the feeble and Friendless, to discountenance the haughty and lawless, to procure Redress of Wrongs, the Advancement of Right, to assert and maintain Liberty and Virtue, to discourage and abolish Tyranny and Vice" (D&A, 1:124).

Such idealism was fostered by the high standards for legal practice in Massachusetts, which developed just as Adams and Sewall were beginning their careers. In place of "pettifoggers," or semiskilled pleaders, a new generation of college graduates emerged, trained in the law offices of learned older men. In 1762 a formal system of training and rank was introduced, along with formalities of gowns and wigs in the Superior Court. In Boston young men had before them the example and inspiration of able judges and seasoned practitioners. Jeremiah Gridley, who first sponsored Adams at the bar, gave him stern counsel to marry late and devote his early years to mastering law as a system of knowledge. He backed up this advice by lending books from his extensive library and later by calling together a "Sodality," or select group for the organized study of law and rhetoric. Adams wrote in his diary on February 21, 1765: "I hope and expect to see, at the Bar, in Consequence of this Sodality, a Purity, an Elegance, and a Spirit, surpassing any Thing that ever appeared in America" (D&A, 1:255).[3] Apart from their laborious study, lawyers also had the steady instruction of arguments in court. They often attended important cases to take notes of the pleadings and their presentation. When the Superior Court went on circuit, they rode together, shared cases, compared strategies, and engaged in long conversations in the lodging houses along the route. And as legal questions often involved constitutional questions in the 1760s and 1770s, the most ambitious men found abundant exercise in thorough research and intricate reasoning.[4]

3. Adams may be directly quoting Gridley in this passage.
4. See Berkin, pp. 10–23; John M. Murrin, "The Legal Transformation: The Bench and Bar of Eighteenth-Century Massachusetts," in *Colonial America: Essays in Politics and Colonial Development*, 3d ed., ed. Stanley N. Katz and John M. Murrin (New York: Knopf, 1983), pp. 540–71; and *Legal Papers of*

Law thus drew these men together through years of shared discipline. And at the heart of their idealism was a conservative reverence for British institutions. Quotations from Adams's letters have already expressed his deep feeling for the excellence of *British* government preserved by the learning and noble spirit of *English* judges. Adams's contemporaries wrote comparable pages of praise. They saw themselves as initiates into the system of justice of the most civilized nation on earth and as guardians of its heritage. They modeled themselves on local men learned in the law and on the English justices whose volumes were their sacred writ.

The years that led up to the Revolution put heavy strains on that devotion. Of fifty-eight lawyers known to have practiced in Massachusetts in 1774, a large number was never reconciled to an independent America. Nineteen left Massachusetts, never to return. A dozen others were known Loyalists who somehow endured, or equivocators who were forced to accept the new order. Five died of causes related to the war, and one or two suffered mental breakdowns.[5] And these numbers tell only part of the story. Legal practice had become a direct route to high office in the provincial government. The great issues of controversy often involved the authority of that government and its courts. Must legal documents be on stamped paper? Should judges receive their salaries from the Crown? Could mob violence or soldiers' crimes be brought to justice through trials by jury? As these questions forced governments to extremities, they forced individual lawyers into anguish. To turn one way or the other meant to betray deep loyalties, fast friendships, and cherished principles.

To study the beginning of the Revolution, therefore, one can hardly do better than read Adams's controversial papers of this time, especially the "Novanglus" papers of 1775. Under this name, Adams wrote thirteen letters to the press, answering a Loyalist who wrote seventeen papers as "Massachusettensis." These cumbersome Latin names mark the papers as ponderous, learned treatises, and both writers do pour forth large reserves of legal and historical information. But both aimed to argue persuasively

---

John Adams, ed. L. Kinvin Wroth and Hiller B. Zobel, 3 vols. (Cambridge Mass.: Harvard University Press, 1965), 1:xxxviii–xciv.

5. I derive these figures from the names and descriptions listed in Adams, *Legal Papers,* 1:xcv–cxiv. John M. Murrin counts twenty-seven avowed Tories or Tory sympathizers among the forty-six Massachusetts barristers of 1774. He also points out that most were over thirty years old and "could not reconcile systematic opposition to royal government with their own devotion to English law" (Murrin, pp. 566–67).

to ordinary citizens. Both were trying to look back to the origins of the controversy that now verged on war and to suggest steps that might heal it. These papers, then, constitute a dramatic public debate about the sources of legitimate government in America—a debate waged by idealistic lawyers who were also skilled writers and, most important, native sons with family roots that reached deep in the local soil. Their contentions and replies at times seem an overture to the war they anticipate. But viewed from another angle they also seem earnest, last-ditch efforts to find a reasoned way from violence back to law. As they project possibilities and probabilities, both writers reveal their blindness to what the future held and even to the chaos that was engulfing them. Two men who might have been close friends here consolidate all they know into contrary versions of American law and right. For Adams, this was to be the summation of his career as a lawyer and a rehearsal for long years of service to a new nation. And for his readers it is still a debate that illuminates his character and its strengths.

Taken together Novanglus and Massachusettensis review a long controversy over the authority of the British Parliament to legislate for the American colonies. In a moment we shall see that this was not the only issue they debated or even the one that both writers regarded as preeminent. But I will first survey how they treat this fundamental problem in order to make clear the contrasts between them.

Reduced to its barest essentials, Massachusettensis' argument holds that in the British system of government the king and Parliament are inseparble; if anything, Parliament is now the supreme authority throughout the British Empire. In recent years, he argues, the colonies have strayed from the true doctrine of subjection to British law. Massachusetts in particular has been led by local demagogues to defy legitimate government. The result has been disorder in the streets, an undermining of the powers of Crown officers, and actions verging on treason—the Boston Tea Party and the calling of provincial and Continental congresses. Britain has now acted properly by sending a military governor and troops to restore order. The mother country has watched with patience and indulgence, but must now act firmly to protect the subjects who have maintained their allegiance to her laws. British rule in the colonies has long been benevolent, and it will be again. But British force is also plainly adequate to control the colonies and punish flagrant crimes.

To all these points Novanglus objects strongly. He holds that the king and Parliament are separate, that the colonists have always been directly subject to the king, and that royal power has been limited by well-established laws and legal procedures. Since representation in Parliament is impractical, the colonies have preserved a different system of internal government, mirroring the balances in the British Constitution of king, Lords, and Commons with their own balances of governor, council, and legislature. It is true that this balance has been jeopardized by recent events. But the fault lies not in the common people or in their leaders but in corrupt British ministers and greedy Massachusetts governors. The latter have worked to concentrate power in their own hands and thus benefit their own fortunes at the cost of others' rights. The solution to this problem is not the imposition of British force, which will not prevail in any case. Rather, the solution lies in a new respect on the part of Parliament and the colonial governors for the fine institutions that are already in place in America. Only by leaving the colonies free to make their own laws within their own borders will the British Empire be strengthened and British liberties preserved.

Condensed and abstracted in this way, the arguments may seem equally persuasive, and so they should. Each of them is informed, consistent, and based on a respectable grasp of fundamental law. From this distance we can see that they articulate two long and distinct lines of political development—a divergence between Britain and America as well as between opposing camps in Massachusetts.

From the time of the first colonization in the early seventeenth century, the British Constitution had undergone major changes. The civil wars, the revolution of 1688, and practical politics under Hanoverian kings had established a new balance between king and Parliament. By 1774 it was clear that George III could not overturn decades of binding precedent. Parliament was the center of British authority; royal prerogative was narrowly limited. A few learned lawyers still argued that Parliament could not enact any law whatever, but they were holdouts against a general understanding of the modern Constitution. Meanwhile, relations had also changed between Britain and the rest of the world, so that a small island realm in northwestern Europe had become a great maritime power with a claim over vast tracts in America and Asia.

In America a different evolution had taken place. Tiny outposts of a few colonists had grown into a thriving seaboard economy. Dozens of town and provincial governments had accustomed the people to participate directly in their own affairs. And the long travel time between the two continents had taught them other important lessons in self-sufficiency. They could supply their own necessities, or they could evade the law and smuggle them in rather handily. They could fight many of their own battles against dangers along their borders. They were educating their own scholars and craftsmen, and projecting their own plans for colonizing the territory to the west. As the calling of the Continental Congress proved, they were on the verge of joining together for concerted action as a large, populous, and energetic domain.

How could two such antagonistic national histories be reconciled by appeal to a common body of laws? What both these writers revealed was that they could not.

The burden of *Massachusettensis* is that the colonies must submit, or they will be coerced to submit by the force of British arms. The first paper opens with that threat and it remains prominent to the end. The writer implies that short of a sudden and unlikely turn of events, any remaining heritage of orderly local self-government will have to give way to a large-scale demonstration of sheer might. He does not quail at the thought of bloodshed. The first paper concludes with an unfavorable forecast of American preparedness, and the seventh, eighth, and ninth papers cast a lurid light on the consequences of rebellion, independence, and involvement in treason.

This argument for force cannot easily be dismissed. If the colonies are subject to Britain and hence to all laws made by Parliament, then it is a straightforward matter of concluding that those laws must be enforced— even by armies from abroad. What is more, it makes good moral sense for a Loyalist who cares about his neighbors to warn them of this danger, especially if he sees the enforcement power as massive and irresistible. Apparently this writer does. He believes that without British government the colonies will be prey to internal disorder and to encroachments from Spain or France—the same dangers that would worry the framers of the

Constitution a dozen years later. Moreover, unpunished crimes, he says, have encouraged further outrages on the road to anarchy. It would be quite wrong to imagine Massachusettensis as either a blustering propagandist or a heartless bully. Like many another Loyalist with a deep longing for order, he feels immense relief that the Boston Tea Party has been answered by the Coercive Acts and other palpable evidence that Britain will take firm action. Yet he still feels duty bound to soften the stroke, to spread an advance warning, and to make clear the justification for chastisement. A terrible judgment is at hand, but he is prepared to call his fellow-men back from the brink: "He that could see his friend persevering in a fatal error, without reminding him of it, and striving to reclaim him, through fear that he might thereby incur his displeasure, would little deserve the sacred name himself," he writes at the opening of his third paper. "Such delicacy is not only false, but criminal. Were I not fully convinced upon the most mature deliberation, that I am capable of, that the temporal salvation of this province depends upon a change of sentiment, respecting our own conduct, and the justice of the British nation, I never should have obtruded myself on the public . . . Should I be so unfortunate as to incur your displeasure, I shall nevertheless think myself happy, if I can snatch but one of my fellow-subjects as a brand out of the burning."[6]

Nevertheless the writer stops short of seeing that armed force could be a cause of rebellion rather than its cure. And he lets slip an important point—that a test of arms has now become the measure of justice. "Upon this point, whether the colonies are distinct states or not, our patriots have rashly tendered Great Britain an issue, against every principle of law and constitution, against reason and common prudence. There is no arbiter between us but the sword; and that the decision of that tribunal will be against us, reason foresees, as plainly as it can discover any event that lies in the womb of futurity" (No. 11, *N&M,* p. 196). Massachusettensis is at pains to show that the patriots are pitting themselves against right as well as might, risking a way of life over inflated grievances. But his words here

---

6. *Novanglus and Massachusettensis* (1819; rpt. New York: Russell & Russell, 1968), pp. 152–53; hereafter cited in the text as *N&M.* I quote from this facsimile of the 1819 edition because it contains both series of essays and includes further related materials by Adams. *Novanglus* is also reprinted in full, including a reconstructed text of number 13 (which Adams never published), in *Papers of John Adams,* ed. Robert J. Taylor (Cambridge, Mass.: Harvard University Press, 1977–), 2:226–387; hereafter cited in text as *Papers.*

undermine the foundations of his argument. If "there is no arbiter between us but the sword," then law has collapsed as a way of settling disputes; reasoned argument is but words shouted against a storm.

Novanglus does not fail to seize on this crucial point. He roundly denies that Parliament can rightfully legislate for the colonies. But even granting—for argument's sake—that the colonies "must be subject to the supreme power of the state," he finds woeful consequences in the situation at hand.

> The consequences that may fairly be drawn are these:—That Britain has been imprudent enough to let the colonies be planted, until they are become numerous and important, without ever having wisdom enough to concert a plan for their government, consistent with her own welfare: that now it is necessary to make them submit to the authority of parliament: and because there is no principle of law or justice, or reason, by which she can effect it; therefore she will resort to war and conquest—to the maxim *delenda est Carthago*. These are the consequences, according to this writer's idea. (No. 7, *N&M*, pp. 84–85)

Novanglus proposes a different solution. After 150 years there is now an evident defect in the arrangements for governing British colonies. This defect "ought to be supplied by some just and reasonable means; that is, by the consent of the colonies; for metaphysicians and politicians may dispute forever, but they will never find any other moral principle or foundation of rule or obedience, than the consent of governors and governed." In other words, the troops now in Boston do not represent a sound and vigorous British policy but rather the cruel last extremity of a failure of policy. If Britain pushes enforcement to the point of armed conflict, she will drive loyal subjects to violence in return and ruin all possibility of stable colonial government.

> She has found out that the great machine will not go any longer without a new wheel. She will make this herself. We think she is making it of such materials and workmanship as will tear the whole machine to pieces. We are willing if she can convince us of the necessity of such a wheel, to assist with artists and materials, in

making it, so that it may answer the end. But she says, we shall have no share in it; and if we will not let her patch it up as she pleases, her Massachusettensis and other advocates tell us, she will tear it to pieces herself, by cutting out throats. To this kind of reasoning we can only answer, that we will not stand still to be butchered. We will defend our lives as long as providence shall enable us. (*N&M*, p. 85)

To forestall such a calamity, Novanglus in his seventh paper outlines new forms of workable government. He would have the colonies assent to parliamentary authority over international affairs. But he would leave internal government, including taxation, to an American congress or to the legislatures of the several provinces. This British system would share allegiance to a common center of authority in the person of the king. But it would safeguard individual liberties by ensuring legislative representation for all territories under the Crown and confining royal prerogative within the bounds of well-drawn charters and established laws.

This plan, however, is riddled with its own contradictions and absurdities. The most obvious is that no one was likely to adopt it. And, almost as devastating, the proposal is all but buried in a complicated legalistic argument. Novanglus goes through paper after paper, piling up citation after citation, to show that Britain has never developed a body of clear constitutional law for governing its colonies. He thus works to blast the contentions for parliamentary supremacy and to exalt the forms of government that had developed through time in the several colonies. But if colonial government is, as he contends, *casus omissus* in established British law, then to what tribunal should a conflict over the colonies be brought? To Parliament, which was already passing the Coercive Acts? To the king, who was assenting to them? To some nonexistent body representative of all British peoples, laws, and interests? It is a good question whether Novanglus himself believes that any solely legal framework can resolve a dispute of this sort. We have just seen him contending for an entirely different source of authority and justice: "Metaphysicians and politicians may dispute forever, but they will never find any other moral principle or foundation of rule or obedience, than the consent of governors and governed." This is strange language for someone who is burrowing his way through tomes of common law, dragging out principles that controlled governors and governed in the reign of James I, and contending that such principles are still binding in 1775.

To a sharp and confident adversary like Massachusettensis, these tangled efforts are simply laughable. "Novanglus strives to hide the inconsistencies of his hypothesis, under a huge pile of learning," he scoffs in his final paper. "Surely he is not to learn, that arguments drawn from obsolete maxims, raked out of the ruins of the feudal system, or from principles of absolute monarchy, will not conclude to the present constitution of government" (*N&M*, p. 226).

Reduced to their central principles, these arguments go round in a perfect stalemate. Both writers would avert violent conflict, though both see it immediately at hand. Both argue like good lawyers, but despair of a legal resolution. The Loyalist insists that the laws will be enforced, though troops are now in Boston because of lawlessness. The Patriot digs and digs to find an unassailable principle of common law and comes up with empty hands, with a *casus omissus*. "There is no arbiter between us but the sword," says Massachusettensis. Novanglus replies that the sword is no arbiter, but a devastating weapon. Novanglus proposes a new arrangement of colonies and Crown, based on a century of evolution and a principle of consent between governors and governed. Massachusettensis replies that this solution is neither constitutional nor practical; it is a mere tissue of whimsy and misplaced erudition. In the present crisis, after deliberate action by king and Parliament, "there is no arbiter between us but the sword."

Many thoughtful cases were made for British authority, and dozens of writers defended American rights during these years. What makes these papers stand out is not their bare doctrines but the peculiar structure that binds them together. Because of the way Novanglus chose to attack his adversary, their papers are almost mirror images of each other. Considering the backgrounds of both authors, their deadlocked opposition is a grotesque perversion of the deepest kind of friendship. It is as though a blade split the New England legal mentality into two symmetrical but contrary attitudes. Page after page they look at the same incidents, laws, public figures, popular moods, and hopes of reconciliation—but all from polar perspectives.

This antagonism shows up plainly in the way *Novanglus* is organized.

Massachusettensis had been writing for over a month, making his case for parliamentary supremacy and answering a number of popular charges against the government, when the first Novanglus paper appeared, dedicated to tracking this adversary and hammering at every one of his contentions and specious claims. The procedure was unrelenting: follow Massachusettensis through each of his papers, quote its main contentions, and then comment at length on their absurdity or falsehood.

Apparently Massachusettensis aimed for a wide popular influence. A pamphlet of the first seven papers was being made up in New York while the others were still being written for the Boston newspapers, and later a full pamphlet of all seventeen papers went through several editions.[7] For all his authoritarian intransigence, the writer presented brief, no-nonsense arguments, well calculated to appeal to ordinary readers.

Why then did Novanglus commit himself to such a complicated form of rebuttal? As it went on it led Adams into a number of awkward tangles. He began clumsily, by attacking the third of the Loyalist's papers, and so had to backtrack to take up his first and second, and then jump ahead to the latter part of the third before going on to the fourth. Because he expatiated at length on his adversary's points, he also moved at a much slower pace. By March he was just beginning to take up papers that had been published in early January. And the Loyalist's sixth paper (for January 16) was to keep Novanglus occupied through five long essays—until newspapers suspended publication in April after war broke out at Lexington and Concord. By that time the Loyalist's series had been drawn to a close, with some strong passages of counterrebuttal. Novanglus seemed to have entered a thicket of obscure, technical points of law, where only a patient expert could follow.

Why should a sensible man, let alone a practiced controversialist like Adams, involve himself in such ineffectual labor? Could he seriously suppose he was preaching to the multitudes? Or that he was pricking the flesh of an opponent who continued with his own assured arguments? Or that he was constructing a synthesis of such depth and logic that it must change the course of empire?

A large part of the answer may lie in a terrible mind set that gripped all

7. Thomas R. Adams, *American Independence* (Providence, R.I.: Brown University Press, 1965), entry 180a–g.

conditions of men as a civil war drew nearer. Neither Loyalist nor Patriot was looking any longer for a point of agreement or shared faith with neighbors who strongly differed. Each was justifying his own cause, trusting nothing he heard from the other side. Centuries earlier Thucydides had noted the same savagery of mind in dozens of city-states torn by revolution. He wrote that as long as human nature remained the same, this meanness would recur: "For in peace and prosperity both states and individuals have gentler feelings, because men are not then forced to face conditions of dire necessity; but war, which robs men of the easy supply of their daily wants, is a rough schoolmaster and creates in most people a temper that matches their condition."[8] Boston in 1775 felt itself on the brink of at least a local war. Loyalists had fled into the protection of the city after their estates and families were threatened by mobs. Some Patriot families, like the Adamses, had prudently moved out, beyond the reach of British troops.

In an earlier day threats and tensions could still be mastered by a civilized, temperate man. Adams recorded that he had had such control in 1768–70, even when British troops were exercised every day in Brattle Square directly in front of his house. "Their very Appearance in Boston was a strong proof to me, that the determination in Great Britain to subjugate Us, was too deep and inveterate ever to be altered by Us: For every thing We could do, was misrepresented, and Nothing We could say was credited." That was one side of his daily reflections. "On the other hand, I had read enough in History to be well aware of the Errors to which the public opinions of the People, were liable in times of great heat and danger, as well as of the Extravagances of which the Populace of Cities were capable, when artfully excited to Passion, and even when justly provoked by Oppression." His own experience in court had reinforced the same lesson. "I had learned enough to shew me, in all their dismal Colours, the deceptions to which the People in their passion, are liable, and the totall Suppression of Equity and humanity in the human Breast when thoroughly heated and hardened by Party Spirit" (*D&A,* 3:290). When urged to harangue public meetings in those years, Adams refused. When soldiers actually did fire on a crowd, in the Boston Massacre, he dutifully

8. Thucydides, *History of the Peloponnesian War,* trans. Charles Forster Smith, Loeb Classical Library (Cambridge, Mass.: Harvard University Press; London: Heinemann, 1930), 2:143.

agreed to defend them in court and secured their acquittals on charges of murder.

But in 1775, after the Tea Party, the Coercive Acts, and the first Continental Congress, the threat at hand was far meaner. It was not Redcoats from overseas or the common people in a passion. It was old friends who could be trusted no longer. It was law courts reorganized by fiat of Parliament. It was the sense that every small concession in Boston would have repercussions throughout the colonies. Now Massachusettensis began his papers charging that all these woes resulted from a long, deep-plotted conspiracy to bring on a revolution. And Novanglus countercharged that the longer, deeper plot was to enslave all of America.

Almost fifty years later it was finally confirmed that *Massachusettensis* had been the work of Daniel Leonard, a lawyer five years younger than Adams and a very recent convert to the Loyalist cause. Until 1773 Leonard had been Adams's close friend and an ally of the other Patriots in the General Court and on the Committee of Correspondence. Then came the Boston Tea Party—which Massachusettensis was to dwell on as an outrage beyond toleration. Adams and others later felt that Leonard had venal motives for changing his loyalties. He was a young man, fond of his chariot and cardplaying and the gold lace on his hat. He was prey to the blandishments of a government that could offer lucrative employment.[9] These charges seem confirmed by the fact that Leonard was promptly rewarded with offices for his writings. But he did not go on to become chief justice of Bermuda and a prosperous barrister of the Inner Temple in London just because of his compliant charm. He also had formidable talents for legal reasoning, which real outrages might have provoked.

Those outrages intensified, once he proclaimed himself. In August 1774 he accepted appointment to the council, and the people of Taunton surrounded his house immediately afterward. Shots were fired through his windows late at night. A month later he, his pregnant wife, and their children fled to the safety of Boston.[10] By January he looked round at an

9. John Adams to Dr. J. Morse, December 22, 1815, in *The Works of John Adams,* ed. Charles Francis Adams, 10 vols. (Boston, 1850–56), 10:194–95.
10. John Langton Sibley and Clifford K. Shipton. *Biographical Sketches of Graduates of Harvard University* (Cambridge, Mass.: Harvard University Press; Boston: Massachusetts Historical Society, 1873-), 14:643–44.

entire province in anarchy. "The occurrences of the summer and autumn past are so recent and notorious," he wrote in his fifth paper, "that a particular detail of them is unnecessary. Suffice it to say that every barrier that civil government had erected for the security of property, liberty and life, was broken down, and law, constitution and government trampled under foot by the rudest invaders" (*N&M,* p. 169).

The spirit behind *Massachusettensis* is therefore complex. It is not merely a hireling's tract. It is an effort at justification, even self-justification, for force as a means to quell a public outrage. Leonard may write with the zeal of a convert, at pains to contradict and overturn even his own past deeds and understandings. But the result is an intelligent series of papers, remarkable for some conciliatory strains. The passage quoted above, about anarchy, is actually bracketed by disciplined understanding: "It is very foreign to my intentions to draw the vengeance of Great Britain upon the whigs; they are too valuable a part of the community to lose, if they will permit themselves to be saved . . . I shall yet become an advocate for the leading whigs; much must be allowed to men, in their situation, forcibly actuated by the chagrin of disappointment, the fear of punishment, and the fascination of hope at the same time" (*N&M,* pp. 168–69).

To Adams, however, such expressions could be only provocative nonsense. Coming from anyone who claimed, as Massachusettensis did, to be a native of the province, writing out of "the most undissembled patriotism" (*N&M,* p. 159), the words stank of smooth hypocrisy. Already Adams had faced down other official attempts to justify abuses of power. Now here was someone he must have known, reasserting all these long demolished arguments. And here were the people of Massachusetts, reading such insidious papers while Patriots throughout the colonies were joining forces to resist manifest tyranny.

Just a few months earlier Adams had confronted the most potent government adversary over these issues. Governor Thomas Hutchinson, in a daring move, had addressed the General Court in 1773, meeting their grievances head-on with a thorough, scholarly review of constitutional principles. Hutchinson too was a native son of the province, a man proud of his comprehensive learning about its history and of his long experience in its councils and courts. His formal address contended that there could be no compromise in interpreting the legal history and status of Massachu-

setts. Either Parliament had supreme authority or the colony really asserted itself as an independent state. To his own satisfaction the governor
felt he had laid a trap for the popular leaders, a presentation of unanswera-
ble logic. But with Adams's help the assembly prepared a full answer and
then a further answer to the governor's reply. These answers were lengthy
and closely reasoned. They quoted the governor's speech verbatim and
adduced much learning to rebut the main points. They even found support
in passages from Hutchinson's own published works.

Politically, if not logically, the Patriots left Hutchinson devastated.
They reprinted and circulated the full text of these exchanges, to show the
world that this governor could be answered, that he was inept in defying
his legislature to a contest on the issues. Later that year he was discredited
in other ways, too. In June his private letters to a correspondent in England were published in a pamphlet—proof, it was claimed, of his long
intrigue against his countrymen. And in December his stubborn refusal to
compromise could be blamed for the crisis that ended in the Tea Party.
Adams and others had long seen Hutchinson as a wily aristocrat, eager to
concentrate offices in the hands of his family and followers and so amass
not only salaries but also special political advantages for their private
interests. Now he stood unmasked. When he sailed for England on June 1,
1774, he left behind a soured reputation. The reasoned case for parliamentary supremacy was tainted with his name.

Who would have the gall to present that case again, with the claim
of disinterested patriotism? Adams was sure he knew. Massachusettensis had to be Jonathan Sewall, the provincial attorney general, Adams's
old friend and frequent public opponent. Forty-five years later, Adams
was still sure of that identification. When the papers were reprinted, he
wrote that in late 1774 "I found the Massachusetts Gazette teeming
with political speculations, and Massachusettensis shining like the moon
among the lesser stars. I instantly knew him to be my friend Sewall,
and was told he excited great exultation among the tories and many
gloomy apprehensions among the whigs. I instantly resolved to enter
the lists with him, and this is the history of the following volume"
(N&M, p. vi). In the first paragraphs of *Novanglus,* Adams insisted that
Sewall had long been a defender of vicious governors and that this
latest series was the last gasp of a hopeless cause.

The public, if they are not mistaken in their conjecture, have been so long acquainted with this gentleman, and have seen him so often disappointed, that if they were not habituated to strange things, they would wonder at his hopes, at this time to accomplish, the most unpromising project of his whole life. In the character of Philanthrop, he attempted to reconcile you to Mr. Bernard. But the only fruit of his labor was, to expose his client to more general examination, and consequently to more general resentment and aversion. In the character of Philalethes, he essayed to prove Mr. Hutchinson a patriot, and his letters not only innocent, but meritorious. But the more you read and considered, the more you were convinced of the ambition and avarice, the simulation and dissimulation, the hypocricy and perfidy of that destroying angel. (*N&M,* pp. 9–10)

The friendship between Adams and Sewall thus came to a climax in these papers. They had long been closely matched rivals as both lawyers and writers. Early in their careers they exchanged letters, already quoted, on their high ideals in the study of law. Soon they were trading blows in the public newspapers. Adams's first letters to the press, his "Humphrey Ploughjogger" papers of 1763, were directly aimed at a series Sewall had written as "J." In 1767 Adams again wrote as Ploughjogger to answer Sewall as "Philanthrop." Sewall still felt close enough to Adams to try to recruit him to a government post, and for some time he seems to have been torn in his own attitudes toward British policies. He refused to prosecute important customs cases against John Hancock, and he left others to prosecute the soldiers for the Boston Massacre.[11] Adams recalled that "he was a gentleman and a scholar; had a fund of wit, humour and satire, which he used with great discretion at the bar, but poured out with unbounded profusion in the newspapers" (*N&M,* p. v). But their friendship was strained by politics until it broke off in July 1774, when both were riding circuit in Maine. Sewall walked out on a hill with Adams and tried to dissuade him from attending the Continental Congress. According to Adams's later account, Sewall used words that could serve as an abstract for *Massachusettensis:* "that Great Britain was determined on her system;

11. Sewall's career is outlined in Berkin; details of his relations with Adams are documented in Adams's *Papers* and *Legal Papers* and the preface to *N&M.*

her power was irresistible and would certainly be destructive to me, and to all those who should persevere in opposition to her designs." Adams replied that he was resolved to go on opposing British injustice. He ended, "I see we must part, and with a bleeding heart I say, I fear forever; but you may depend upon it, this adieu is the sharpest thorn on which I ever sat my foot" (*N&M,* p. vi).

Massachusettensis and *Novanglus* seem to have intensified this breach between comrades. If Adams saw Sewall as the Loyalist author, how could he avoid feeling that this case was addressed almost personally to himself? And how could Adams, who had answered Sewall many times before, resist the challenge to counterattack? The dogged animus that seized on *Massachusettensis* and tried to shake every part of every paper may have had this complex motive. It was partly a way of focusing Adam's tense hatred for Hutchinson and all the ruin his machinations had caused, but it was also a way of working through a bitter parting, by refusing to yield the last word.[12]

And there was a further strength that, at this point, Adams could show. When he and Sewall said farewell, Adams was on the point of leaving for the Continental Congress. When he began to write *Novanglus,* he had just returned. The experience in Philadelphia, a new one for him, had confirmed his convictions. He rode out of New England for the first time in his life and found himself the equal, and soon one of the leaders, of dozens of like-minded men from other colonies. He began to form new bonds to replace the friendships broken off with Boston Loyalists. In October he was asked to work out the crucial section of a Declaration of Rights and Grievances, the carefully worded fourth article defining the authority of Parliament:

That the foundation of English liberty, and of all free government, is a right in the people to participate in their legislative council: and as the English colonists are not represented, and from their local and other circumstances, cannot be properly represented in the British parliament, they are entitled to a free and exclusive power of legislation in their several provincial legislatures, where their right of repre-

12. Another strain may be Adams's habit of dashing off angry answers to many of Sewall's writings. Some of these first drafts are full of raw invective. See Adams, *Papers,* 1:62–63, 176–78.

sentation can alone be preserved, in all cases of taxation and internal polity, subject only to the negative of their sovereign, in such manner as has been heretofore used and accustomed. But, from the necessity of the case, and a regard to the mutual interest of both countries, we cheerfully consent to the operation of such acts of the British parliament, as are bona fide, restrained to the regulation of our external commerce, for the purpose of securing the commercial advantages of the whole empire to the mother country, and the commercial benefits of its respective members; excluding every idea of taxation, internal or external, for raising a revenue on the subjects in America, without their consent. (*Papers,* 2:160–61)

Here was a compact summary of the main argument to be developed in *Novanglus:* that free government must rest on consent. And here it came not only from Adams's own pen but from his shared deliberations with other constitutional thinkers. Returning to Boston, reinforced by this experience, Adams was prepared to see through anyone's threats with renewed conviction that justice lay with the Patriots. He must also have sensed that what he argued hereafter would be noticed on a wider stage. Thus Adams had reason to believe that *Novanglus* could win a real victory, even if it failed to move his adversaries in Boston. It might reach like-minded Americans there or elsewhere and reinforce their persuasion by penetrating the depths of English law on the matter at hand.

Still, Adams seems to have been blind to the indifference of common readers and to the impervious set of the Loyalist mind. He went on, week after week, as though his attacks on his opponent were having the desired effects. Public tension, personal grief, long-standing disillusionment with the government, and new-found confirmation all help to explain Adams's energetic performance. But in the end, he produced papers that are almost self-defeating. They are involved so inextricably with *Massachusettensis* that each argument perpetually sticks to the other. There is no way to fully appreciate Adams except in the terms first provided by Hutchinson, Leonard, and Sewall. Even Adams's most sympathetic reader has to limit his assent because of this form. He has to read both series assiduously until he sees them not as victor and vanquished but as Whig and Tory twins.

To anyone interested in the Revolution, these matched sets of papers are all the more revealing because their deadlock is so complete, in both doctrine and form. They show a convinced Loyalist and a convinced patriot exchanging point for point, explaining different ways of seeing the same masses of fact and history. Indeed they show how each side could understand and face its opposite. Other efforts to comprehend both sides were also being made around this time. Jonathan Sewall did not write *Massachusettensis,* but in 1775 he did publish a little play to dramatize the Loyalist persuasion. And long before, in 1768, Governor Hutchinson privately labored over a dialogue, in which he tried to meet the full and stirring arguments of a brilliant Patriot. *Novanglus* and *Massachusettensis* can be best appreciated by comparing them to these other attempts to achieve a balanced argument.

Sewall's little drama reveals the playful side of his mind that Adams admired, the profusion of a well-read wit. The title page quotes a motto from Horace, on mingling delight with instruction, and the title promises relief from the labor of heavy thinking: *A Cure for the Spleen, or Amusement for a Winter's Evening; Being the Substance of a Conversation on the Times, over a friendly Tankard and Pipe.*[13] The scene is a country house; the characters, a handful of stock comedians: Sharp, the parson; Bumper, a country justice; Fillpot, the innkeeper; Graveairs, a deacon; Trim, a barber; Brim, a Quaker; and Puff, a late representative in the General Court. All their talk is supposed to have been taken down in shorthand by the famous justice of Addison's *Spectator,* Sir Roger de Coverly.

The play turns out to be a vehicle for the teaching of Parson Sharp, the host and chief talker. The other characters reveal themselves as ignorant rustics, who often talk about politics but understand it no better than Greek. Undaunted by their shallowness, Sharp proceeds to explain the Massachusetts Charter and parliamentary laws since 1650 and to answer and ridicule common fears and rumors about parliamentary power. His speeches are interrupted and redirected by questions and jokes. But he says enough to convince his hearers; in the end they all agree to either change their thinking or be quiet.

13. I quote from the edition in the *Magazine of History* 20, no. 3, extra no. 79 (1922), 119–55; page references hereafter cited in the text.

The theme of this work, like that of *Massachusettensis,* is that British power is irresistible and the Patriots are wrong in opposing it. But the form is very simple. Sewall seems so convinced of his case that he cannot imagine an intelligent objection. Demagogues and poor dupes are all that the Whigs amount to, and the sooner the common people learn the plain facts the better. "It is enough to make a wise man mad," says Bumper, "to see how tamely the common people suffer themselves to be fooled, first out of their senses, and then out of their *liberty, property,* and *lives*" (p. 150). The play goes on in that vein for pages; it seems to have been produced as an easy tract for the nearly converted.

Hutchinson's dialogue is much more serious, for it presents two trenchant opponents who evidently learn from each other in the course of their arguments. It even shows the Patriot spokesman raising questions and problems that are not adequately answered before the manuscript breaks off. Hutchinson may have begun this piece with the idea of producing a pamphlet, but he never finished it and it remained ignored among his papers for over two centuries. When it was again brought to light a few years ago, it helped reestablish the author as an anguished thinker instead of the selfish turncoat his enemies thought him.[14] Hutchinson does not freely imagine a case for the Patriots. Rather, he synthesizes a strong argument for independence from Parliament out of pamphlets and petitions that had been circulating since the Stamp Act crisis; he even provides footnotes to some of these sources. The dialogue therefore anticipates the complexities of Adams and Leonard, and sees through their deadlock better than they do.

The crucial question stands out in the middle of the dialogue: "But who is to be the judge?" (p. 389). Hutchinson explores this problem as a moral dilemma as well as a constitutional one. The Patriot holds that some parts of the British Constitution are so fundamental that even Parliament cannot violate them. "These fundamentals set bounds to Parliamentary power, and the great oracle of the English law, Lord Coke, says in his Reports that acts made against the fundamental principles of the constitution are

---

14. Thomas Hutchinson, "A Dialogue between an American and a European Englishman," ed. Bernard Bailyn, *Perspectives in American History* 9 (1975): 343–410; page references hereafter cited in the text. This dialogue is also discussed at length in Bailyn, *The Ordeal of Thomas Hutchinson* (Cambridge, Mass: Harvard University Press, 1974), pp. 99–108.

void" (p. 390). The Patriot implies—as some theorists believed Coke did—that a proper law court would set such laws aside. As examples of inviolable principles the Patriot cites the British subject's right to dispose of property only by his own consent—that is, to taxation only through representation. In reply, the Loyalist shows that there are subjects even in England—such as the Catholics—who must pay heavy taxes with no hope of representation. He states that property and consent are not the deepest principles. "Indeed, I know of no principle in the English constitution more fundamental and which is more certain always to remain than this, viz., that no act can be made or passed in any Parliament which it shall not be in the power of a subsequent Parliament to alter and repeal. You will find this in the same author, Lord Coke, whom you cite to show that acts contrary to fundamentals are void" (pp. 401–02). This view unfolds to become the modern doctrine that only Parliament can determine what is fundamental and that, by letting stand or altering its own laws, Parliament determines what is just.

But by this point the Patriot has shifted ground, to give up law courts for private conscience:

> Notwithstanding all you have said, I can easily conceive that there may be certain fundamental principles of government and that the people of which such government is constituted are freed from all obligation to subjection when the supreme authority departs from these fundamentals, and as we know no government which has constituted an umpire or judge to determine when these principles are departed from, every man's own conscience must be the judge and he must follow the evidence of truth in his own mind and submit or not submit accordingly. (p. 399)

At first the Loyalist dismisses this notion as absurd: there must be a sovereign power in any government, a power capable of making and enforcing its laws even by coercing individuals who object for any reason. But as the argument continues, he too shifts his ground. At one point he allows that a judge, persuaded of the injustice of a law, should abandon the bench rather than execute it. Later he allows that a rebellion may be stirred up for principles that are morally right, though the rebels must run the risk of being found legally guilty if they fail of success. As the dialogue breaks off, he concedes that "laws against the general bent of the people, I agree with you, cannot long continue in the English constitution."

The rough state of this manuscript seems to reflect the fluid state of Hutchinson's private thinking. His character's exchanges do not firmly point to a fixed conclusion. Leonard's and Adams's ideas are embedded in the dialogue, but they are softened in a context of mutual concession. Late in the manuscript the Patriot comes out with a compact statement of what he wants:

> We propose that no taxes should be laid upon us but by our own legislatures, that we should be governed in general by laws of our making, but in matters of commerce we are willing to be restrained by acts of the British Parliament, for as we depend upon you for protection against the other powers of Europe we do not think it reasonable that we should carry on trade beneficial to them and detrimental to you. (p. 407)

These words could pass for a draft of Adam's fourth article in the 1774 Declaration of Rights and Grievances. The Loyalist replies that such a plan will never suffice. Already customs laws over external commerce are being flagrantly defied; at each concession by Parliament the Patriots will only insist on more. The more direct solution is force. Like Massachusetensis, the Loyalist foresees quick capitulation to a decided British policy. "One ship of war in each of your principal ports, with such powers as in your case would be no more than reasonable, would reduce every colony in a very few months." The Patriot's words at this point would do an Adams credit: "You may find it more difficult than you imagine" (p. 408). Yet these threats and retorts are here spoken in the same breath with reassurances of good feeling. "You are Englishmen," the Loyalist jokes heartily. "No people upon the globe have been oftener in a frenzy and none sooner return to their senses." And the Partriot almost agrees that the people have been put in a frenzy by leaders no sensible man would trust. Altogether these last few pages of the dialogue reveal a startling development. Both of the characters retain their opposing ideas of right, yet both have moved away from legalistic arguments and are allowing wide areas of genial agreement. It is as though, by moving from principles of law to problems of political conscience, they have grown more respectful of each other as puzzled fellow beings. Each has come to internalize this conflict, just as over his private desk Hutchinson himself seems to have done.

It is hard to imagine Thomas Hutchinson bringing such balanced openness into effective public notice. By 1768 he was already too deeply implicated in government offices to make any believable or tolerable gesture of concession. After he became governor in 1770 he was even more constricted by his public role.

The same must be admitted of *Massachusettensis* and *Novanglus*. Leonard and Adams, too, were locked into unyielding public roles in these series. But the form they took required that they pay close attention to each other and hold out some recognition of a common heritage. Leonard, as we have seen, could no longer joke about the Patriots as fellow Englishmen. To his mind, they had gone too far into open rebellion. But he still saw their leaders as too valuable to lose; he still wanted to save many a brand from the burning. Adams was even stingier about what he would concede to the Tories. But by answering Massachusettensis as minutely as he did, he implied that there was still some framework in which a fair judge could impose a binding decision on them both.

In fact, it is in this light that *Novanglus* best makes sense—if it is read not as a pamphlet or an address to the public but as an appellate case before a wise, noble, and discerning British bench. Call it persistence of professional habit, or undying idealism, or willful obliteration of the recent collapse of the Massachusetts charter: Adams goes on imagining himself not in a play, a dialogue, or a deliberative debate but in a grand court of law where a final demonstrative case can be made and affirmed.

This imagery still shaped Adams's recollections over forty years later. In 1818 he wrote a series of long letters recalling early legal disputes that, he felt, gave birth to the Revolution. He focused particularly on the pleading of James Otis, Jr., in the famous *Writs of Assistance* case of 1761. Adams wrote out a full recollection of Otis's argument—in eighteen consecutive letters!—and framed it in a description of the law court in which it was proclaimed. His letter of March 29, addressed to his former law clerk William Tudor, asks if he can find a painter, perhaps Colonel Trumbull, to recapture this splendid court.

The scene is the council chamber of the old town house in Boston. The date is the month of February, 1761, nine years before you came to me in Cole lane. . . .

That council chamber was as respectable an apartment, and more so too, in proportion, than the house of lords or house of commons in Great Britain, or that in Philadelphia in which the declaration of independence was signed in 1776.

In this chamber, near the fire, were seated five judges, with lieutenant governor Hutchinson at their head, as chief justice; all in their new fresh robes of scarlet English cloth, in their broad bands, and immense judicial wigs. In this chamber was seated at a long table all the barristers of Boston, and its neighbouring county of Middlesex, in their gowns, bands and tye-wigs. They were not seated on ivory chairs; but their dress was more solemn and more pompous than that of the Roman Senate, when the Gauls broke in upon them. . . .

Two portraits, at more than full length, of king Charles the second, and king James the second, in splendid golden frames, were hung up in the most conspicuous side of the apartment. If my young eyes or old memory have not deceived me, these were the finest pictures I have seen. The colours of their long flowing robes and their royal ermines were the most glowing, the figures the most noble and graceful, the features the most distinct and characteristic: far superior to those of the king and queen of France in the senate chamber of congress. . . . One circumstance more. Samuel Quincy and John Adams had been admitted barristers at that term. John Adams was the youngest. He should be painted, looking like a short thick fat archbishop of Canterbury, seated at the table, with a pen in his hand, lost in admiration. (*N&M,* pp. 244–45)

Adams goes on to call attention to three principal actors in this scene. The chief justice, Hutchinson, here is accused of taking this office with prejudiced intentions, "for the direct purpose of deciding this question in favour of the crown, and all others in which it should be interested" (*N&M,* p. 246). The government lawyer was Jeremiah Gridley, who had trained Otis and sponsored Adams, and whom Adams calls "the father of the bar in Boston" at this period (*N&M,* p. 239). Here he argued "with his characteristic learning, ingenuity and dignity"; but his case hung on one dangerous premise—that the Parliament of Great Britain was the sovereign legislature of all the British Empire (*N&M*, p. 246). Against these formidable opponents the chief pleader was Otis—and "Otis was a flame of Fire! With a promptitude of classical allusions, a depth of research, a rapid summary of historical events and dates, a profusion of legal authorities, a prophetic glare of his eyes into futurity, and a rapid torrent of eloquence he hurried away all before him" (*N&M*, p. 246). As Adams concludes this narrative, the judges were driven into a corner by Otis's power. They delayed judgment, admitted that Otis's case seemed to prevail, wrote to England for further information on this constitutional issue, and never revealed any reply. In short, as early as 1761, a brilliant lawyer showed the way to bring constitutional questions before the bar of high British justice and prevail against usurpations by Parliament.

It need hardly be pointed out that Adams is here creating myth, not history. Many details of this great "scene" are inaccurate, and he exaggerates its importance in a ringing line: "Then and there the child Independence was born" (*N&M*, p. 246). But as a myth the scene still has its value as a clue to Adams's own cast of mind. A sharp Patriot faces a learned opponent in front of a hostile judge, and wins his case on its undeniable merits. The same pattern recurs in another letter where Samuel Adams faces Hutchinson and Colonel Dalrymple in this same great chamber after the Boston Massacre, and by cool legal reasoning forces them to evacuate all regular troops out of the town (*N&M*, pp. 259–61). And this same pattern seems to inform *Novanglus*. His letters describing these "scenes" were appended to the edition of *Novanglus and Massachusettensis* that he helped prepare in 1819. And his final paragraph as Novanglus points to a legal victory. He claims that all his tortuous research demolishes his adversary's case; it proves that Parliament has no claim to sovereignty over the colonies.

> Let me now dismiss this [Massachusettensis] Paper of January the Sixteenth. It contains the Ground, the Principle and Foundation of the whole Building. It is an Attempt to prove the Supream Authority of Parliament by the Constitution. But it is the feeblest, the most frivolous, the weakest, the most absurd, Effort that ever was made. One would have thought that a Master Builder would have laid his Corner

Stone to the best of his skill. Without the constitutional Authority contended for in this Paper, all the other Writings of Massachusettensis are mere Harrangue. Whoever reads it, and considers it, will be convinced how easy it is for any Scribbler on the side of Power, by Means of the Court Trumpetters to get a Reputation; and that this Man, however he has been cryed up for a Wit and Humourist and altho' he is a pretty popular Declaimer, is not the most knowing Man in the World, in the grounds of this great Controversy. (*Papers,* 2:385)

In other words, the government case is not a case at all, and any wise judge would throw it out of court.

Perhaps Adams even held some slight faith that its author would change his mind. He claimed that he had seen that kind of miracle, too, in the *Writs of Assistance* case. Otis treated his mentor Gridley with all the deference and esteem of a son to a father "while he baffled and confounded all his authorities, and confuted all his arguments and reduced him to silence." In return, "Mr. Gridley himself seemed to me to exult inwardly at the glory and triumph of his pupil" (*N&M,* pp. 274, 288).

Of course, there was no great court Adams could now appeal to, and we must doubt that Leonard or Sewall exulted inwardly at the sight of *Novanglus.* But by working through his brief, Adams completed his own conviction of Tory self-contradiction and injustice. It would still be a few months before he could take the further step of openly declaring for independence.[15] But here we can see him preparing to do that while grasping at the last evaporating shadows of British legal wisdom.

The story of *Novanglus* thus reveals a number of acute minds, all struggling with the puzzle of how to name themselves. Were they British or American or something in between? If they were Patriots, what was their *patria;* if servants of the government, which was the legitimate government? Hutchinson, when he wrote his dialogue, had to call his interlocutors something. He named them "American" and "European" and so composed "A Dialogue between an American and a European Englishman."[16] Leonard, a few years later, identified himself as a learned native son. He took the name

15. Robert J. Taylor, "John Adams: Legalist as Revolutionist," Massachusetts Historical Society, *Proceedings,* 89 (1977): 55–71, esp. pp. 67–69.
16. Hutchinson, "Dialogue," p. 368.

of the province—derived from the local Indians—and flourished it in jawbreaking scholarly Latin: Massachusettensis. Adams completed this process with something like a pun. Novanglus—New Englander—or New Englishman, a man proud of his British liberty in the New World.

Writing under that name and all that it meant, Adams stood his ground. He became a stalwart defender of the British Constitution as a way into helping shape the American. And in an epilogue to these events, he had the chance to pick up these threads of experience and help define a new relationship with Great Britain after the war.

Congress chose him to be the first American minister to the British court, and on June 1, 1785, he presented his credentials to George III. London newspapers sneered at this situation. Adams too was nervous that the king might not receive a former traitor, one whom the privy council had singled out as exempt from pardon. But in good court dress, prepared with correct protocol and a memorized speech, Adams bowed his way into the royal presence. He thus moved alone into the great court scene he had once imagined. Before him was not the gilt-framed, ermine-clad image of Charles II or James II, but the living king that Adams had once regarded as the sovereign source of justice. Both the king and the American minister were agitated by this meeting; both were gracious and cordial in recognizing the occasion to renew deep bonds of kindred blood. But Adams was now a confirmed American. As he reported to John Jay the next day, the king went on to unbend a little, asking if Adams had not just come from France.

> He put on an air of familiarity, and, smiling, or rather laughing, said, "there is an opinion among some that you are not the most attached of all your countrymen to the manners of France." I was surprised at this, because I thought it an indiscretion and a departure from the dignity. I was a little embarrassed, but determined not to deny the truth on one hand, nor leave him to infer from it any attachment to England on the other. I threw off as much gravity as I could, and assumed an air of gayety and a tone of decision as far as was decent, and said, "that opinion, sir, is not mistaken; I must avow to your Majesty, I have no attachment but to my own country." The king replied, as quick as lightning, "an honest man will never have any other."[17]

17. Adams to John Jay, June 1, 1785, in Adams, *Works,* 8:258. See also *D&A,* 3:422–23.

4

Cato at Valley Forge

The warfare of the American Revolution has long been identified with the courage, sacrifice, dignity, skill, and endurance of one man: His Excellency George Washington, general and commander in chief of the American armed forces. From the first establishment of an army by Congress until the final withdrawal of the British from New York harbor, Washington was the central figure in this great drama. His name was probably better known that any other leader's, and because he traveled widely and conspicuously through America, his face was familiar to thousands of his countrymen at the same time that his orders and actions affected their lives.

But, even now, it is difficult to glimpse the living man within the stereotyped images: the horseman riding past in uniform, the tall man standing in a studied pose in the famous full-length portrait. Perhaps it is because we see only various strands of his personality, depending on where we look, that we fail to see him whole.

In one aspect, for example, Washington was uniquely prepared for a great command. He was a large man and a superb horseman, imbued from an early age with courage and a sense of duty. He also developed early habits of smooth formality and stern self-assertion as a slaveholding Virginia planter and militia officer. His papers show this identity clearly. To inferiors he gives commands in plain, unequivocal prose, with the consequences of disobedience spelled out. To superiors and near equals, he nicely balances deference with a belief in his own worth and dignity. In his twenties and thirties—the ages when Franklin was pushing a wheelbarrow through the streets and Adams was poring over law books by lamplight—Washington was facing insolent French officers and Indians on the frontier, signing death warrants for deserters, stipulating to British merchants exactly how cargoes of stylish goods were to be shipped to Mount Vernon, and negotiating rapid promotions and very large land speculations. He grew rich and powerful by careful management, and the result is there for anyone to read. His letters leave no doubt that this was a man to be reckoned with.

Yet in the long sweep of the Revolution, his power to command often seems trivial or even fortuitous. Through long seasons he headed armies that were on the verge of disintegration—lacking ammunition; lacking clothing, food, shelter, and medicine; lacking training, discipline, or even common decency. Washington himself survived through astonishing good luck. An early case of smallpox incurred on a trip to the West Indies inoculated him against a disease that decimated his troops. He rode untouched out of battles that killed or maimed officers around him. Rivals who might have challenged his supremacy fell away in the course of time. His inexperience in a large command turned out to be an asset in an unorthodox war—although at the cost of severe losses and some near-disasters. In the end he won a glorious victory over Cornwallis at Yorktown, but only with the massive support (and prodding) of French forces on land and sea. Although Washington's talents made a difference, they are difficult to trace through accounts of eight years of complicated, scattered warfare. Sometimes a reader is struck by an almost grotesque disparity between his glittering fineness and the dirty skirmishes of his sick and tattered amateurs.

To complicate matters further, there is the vexing question of how Washington saw himself. At times the professional soldier, he insisted on every nuance of military etiquette, well aware that he and his officers embodied the American cause. He *was* his uniform and he demanded respect for it—from Congress, the states, and foreign powers. At other times he was just as clearly the citizen-soldier, a gentleman who stepped out of Congress and, refusing any salary, put on his sword against his own inclination. He wore his uniform like a costume, to be laid aside as soon as possible. Furthermore, Washington's experience of the business of soldering was wide ranging. It encompassed personal hardships and risks in small-scale frontier combat, intrigue among jealous officers, ingenious strategy in novel situations, and tedious paperwork to persuade slow civilian legislatures and coordinate complicated chains of command.

To look at Washington in the Revolution, then, is to look through a kaleidoscope at a figure that will not be still. But perhaps we can discern the several strands of his personality by concentrating on one small incident that occurred in medias res. On May 11, 1778, Joseph Addison's *Cato* was staged for officers of the Continental Army at Valley Forge. Judging from an eyewitness report, it would seem that the play was put on as an entertainment, part of a festive evening as the awful winter gave way to spring and a new campaign. But other evidence supplementing that single report indicates that when General Washington and his companions sat down to hear Addison's verses, they were prepared to find in them an apt account of their own condition. The figures on stage and the living soldiers who beheld them reflected and complemented one another. To recount this performance and its background is therefore to see an old verse tragedy coming alive in a new setting, finding an audience attuned to its possibilities and embodying ideas the audience celebrated as its own.

The words *Valley Forge* have come to symbolize a good part of the American Revolution. Literally, of course, they name a small settlement near Philadelphia, where Washington's army survived the harsh winter of 1777–78. Metaphorically they have come to stand for a valley or low point in the war. The encampment lay midway in time and space between Bunker Hill and Yorktown, and it was here that the army came close to disintegrating. Yet it somehow endured and was "forged" into new strength for eventual victory.

The camp was settled in late December with some of its rough huts not completed until mid-January. Washington chose the site because it was well defended but still close enough to Philadelphia that he could keep an eye on the British. He soon found, however, that it was almost barren of necessary supplies. On December 23 he wrote to the Congress that "unless some great and capital change suddenly takes place . . . this Army must inevitably be reduced to one or other of these three things. Starve, dissolve, or disperse in order to obtain subsistence." To prove that he was not exaggerating, he reported that there was already a threat of mutiny; that there was no meat to be had and only twenty-five barrels of flour; that there were almost three thousand men "now in Camp unfit for duty because they are bare foot and otherwise naked"; that lacking blankets, many huddled by campfires through the night. The same conditions, compounded by disease, crowding, and the despair of looking anywhere else for relief, were still filling Washington's letters in February.[1]

The general exhorted his men to endurance. "He persuades himself," read the General Orders for December 17, "that the officers and soldiers, with one heart, and one mind, will resolve to surmount every difficulty, with a fortitude and patience, becoming their profession, and the sacred cause in which they are engaged. He himself will share in the hardship, and partake of every inconvenience" (*Writings,* 10:168). But sleeping in the cold was only part of Washington's humiliation. While he was at Valley Forge, the British were living in splendor in Philadelphia, and there were many annoying reminders that the recent campaign had been far from glorious. Congressmen and members of the Pennsylvania legislature were vocal in their complaints. After three years of war, Washington had failed to strike a decisive blow; he had had to give up both New York and Philadelphia. The year before in the dead of winter he had made his stunning moves across the Delaware and on to Princeton, to shock the British and reclaim control of New Jersey. Now here he was shivering among forces incapable of fighting while other commanders encroached on his authority. General Horatio Gates was a sudden hero for his capture of Burgoyne's army at Saratoga in October. Around the same time, an upstart named Thomas Conway persuaded Congress to commission him a major general, with orders to review the discipline of all the armies. Washington soon discovered that Conway was writing to Gates: "Heaven has been determind to save your Country; or a weak General and bad Councellors would have ruind it" (*Writings,* 10:29). There may never have been a Conway "cabal" organized to topple Washington in favor of a new commander. But Washington had to struggle for months with the

---

1. *Writings of George Washington,* ed. John C. Fitzpatrick, 39 vols. (Washington, D.C.: U.S. Government Printing Office, 1931–44), 10:187, 192–94, 469; hereafter cited as *Writings.*

knowledge that his supremacy was being defied if not undermined—in Congress, at Gates's headquarters, wherever Conway might be active.

After mid-February, however, the worst was over. Food, clothing, and other provisions began to arrive. Washington's backbiters did no more than embarrass themselves. The sun came out, and men who had survived the ordeal were linked in a new solidarity. Late in February the self-styled Frederick William Augustus Henry Ferdinand, Baron von Steuben, arrived and proved that he had genuine talents as a drillmaster. He introduced new discipline into the troops and gave an extraordinary boost to their morale. One of his aides, Pierre Etienne Du Ponceau, later recalled good times growing out of hardship.

> We who lived in good quarters did not feel the misery of the times so much as the common soldiers and the subaltern officers, yet we had more than once to share our rations with the sentry at our door. We put the best face we could upon the matter. Once with the Baron's permission, his aids invited a number of young officers to dine at our quarters, on condition that none should be admitted that had on a whole pair of breeches. This was understood, of course, as *pars pro toto,* but torn clothes were an indispensible requisite for admission and in this the guests were very sure not to fail. The dinner took place; the guests clubbed their rations, and we feasted sumptuously on tough beef steaks and potatoes with hickory nuts for our dessert. In lieu of wine, we had some kind of spirits with which we made *Salamanders;* that is to say, after filling our glasses, we set the liquor on fire, and drank it up flame and all. Such a set of ragged and, at the same time, merry fellows were never before brought together. The Baron loved to speak of that dinner, and of his *sans culottes* as he called us. Thus the denomination was first invented in America, and applied to the brave officers and soldiers of our revolutionary army, at a time when, it could not be foreseen, that the name which honoured the followers of Washington would afterwards be assumed by the satellites of a Marat and a Robespierre.[2]

2. "The Autobiography of Peter Stephen Du Ponceau," *Pennsylvania Magazine of History and Biography* 63 (1939): 208; hereafter cited in the text as "Du Ponceau."

Soon Martha Washington and other officers' wives and daughters arrived and lightened the evenings. "There were no *levees* or formal soirees: no dancing, card-playing, or amusements of any kind except singing. Every gentlemen or lady who could sing was called upon in turn for a song" ("Du Ponceau," p. 209).

At the end of April news arrived that completely changed the prospects of the war: France had recognized American independence and offered a treaty of alliance. Already an impulse toward celebration was at work in the camp, matched by a relaxed mood at headquarters. The journal of George Ewing, a young artillery officer, provides the details.[3] On April 15, Ewing "receivd a ticket for the Play to be acted this evening at the Bakehouse" and went, only to discover that the house was so full that he could not get in. (No other report of this play is known.) The news from France arrived on April 30. The next morning the soldiers celebrated with May Day pageantry.

> Last Evening May poles were Erected in everry Regt in the Camp and at the Revelle I was awoke by three cheers in honor of King Tamany. The day was spent in mirth and Jollity, the soldiers parading, marching with fife & Drum, and Huzzaing as they passed the poles, their hats adornd with white blossoms.

At length thirteen platoons of thirteen privates each were drawn up and marched to headquarters to do honor to Washington. He sent word that he was indisposed, but the men retired "with the greatest decency and regularity," and other officers treated them generously with whiskey, song, and dance. Three days later, "His Excellency dined with G Nox [General Henry Knox] and after dinner did us the honor to play at Wicket with us."

When Washington could officially announce the treaty with France, he set May 6 aside as a day of rejoicing throughout the army. Prisoners convicted at courts-martial were granted pardons. An elaborate *feu de joye* was arranged, in which cannon salutes were followed by a running fire of musketry for each of three formal cheers—to the king of France, the friendly European powers, and the American states. This was a chance to

3. Thomas Ewing, *George Ewing, Gentlemen: A Soldier of Valley Forge* (Yonkers, N.Y.: privately printed, 1928). Quotations are cited by date rather than page, and I have supplied some punctuation.

display both plentiful ammunition and the new precision achieved under Steuben. Officers then assembled in an outdoor amphitheater where Washington had ordered an entertainment—band music, a feast, and wine for formal toasts. "The General himself wore a countenance of uncommon delight and complacence," wrote a correspondent from the camp; and someone who had detected a spy during the day was advised to say nothing about it: the spy's report would give the enemy more grief than his being caught and hanged.[4]

Five days later, in the afterglow of this military pride and ceremony, Washington's officers staged Addison's *Cato.*

The play is little read today, even in graduate courses on neoclassical drama. But in the eighteenth century it was performed often and celebrated as the major work of a great moralist. It also became familiar in both England and America as a collection of stirring speeches about virtue, patriotism, and courage against overwhelming tyranny.

The play represents the final day in the life of Cato, the stern Roman patriot who fell on his sword at Utica when he saw the republic and his own forces yielding to the power of Caesar. It is written in blank verse, strictly observes the unities of time and place, and seems designed to project a classic example of classic virtue. The hero is presented as an awesome example of stately wisdom and self-sacrifice. Cato was long a favorite hero of the ancient world. Dante presents him as the guardian of Purgatory, the master of Free Will, or liberty. And Swift, in *Gulliver's Travels* (Book 3, chap. 7) counts him among a half-dozen supreme wise men and martyrs, including Brutus, Socrates, and Sir Thomas More, "a *sextumvirate* to which all the ages of the world cannot add a seventh." But vivid details from sources like Plutarch and Cicero were left out of Addison's script and the result is an uncompromising stiffness. When Addison wrote his *Spectator* papers, he had his own second thoughts about this hero. In one paper he called Stoicism "the pedantry of virtue" (No. 243); in others he suggested that Cato's character was "rather awful than amiable" and might have been improved by some tincture of good nature (Nos. 169, 557).

4. *Pennsylvania Packet,* May 13, 1778, quoted in *The Feu de Joye,* comp. John Baer Stoudt (Norristown, Pa.: Norristown Press, 1928), p. 16.

Addison's manuscript lay unfinished and seen only by a few of his friends until 1713 and the end of Queen Anne's reign. Then it was rapidly completed and brought on stage to meet the crisis of contemporary politics. Addison's friends prevailed upon him, according to an early biographer, "to put the last finishing to it, at a time when they thought the doctrine of Liberty very seasonable."[5] Addison asked John Hughes to write the fifth act and then completed it himself. He took advice from Lady Mary Wortley Montagu about details of the language and appeals to liberty. He enlarged a subplot of young lovers, star-crossed by the demands of duty. And he allowed Richard Steele to pack the theater with a claque for the opening performances.[6]

The result was a great success at Drury Lane, but Addison might have wondered in private what he had really achieved. Although he usually tried to hold aloof from party squabbles, he soon found himself at the center of a political embarrassment. Whigs and Tories competed in applauding key lines of the play, and one night the Tories gathered up fifty guineas and made a theatrical coup of their own against Marlborough. They presented the purse to Booth, the leading actor, for "defending the cause of Liberty so well against a perpetual dictator" (Smithers, p. 265). At another extreme, Addison the critic had to see his own work ruthlessly anatomized. John Dennis published a thorough examination of failings in plot, character, and language from the opening scenes onward. A reader puzzled by *Cato* can still find an hour's relief and instruction in Dennis's malicious commentaries.[7]

The play survived a change of seasons even so and went on holding audiences long after Addison died and old political issues were forgotten. Late in the century Dr. Johnson printed several pages of Dennis's criticism in his own *Life of Addison,* but he decided that the public was right to appreciate *Cato.* It was "rather a poem in dialogue than a drama," he wrote, "rather a succession of just sentiments in elegant language than a repre-

---

5. *The Miscellaneous Works of Joseph Addison,* ed. A. C. Guthkelch, 2 vols. (London: G. Bell and Sons, 1914), 1:xx. Quotations from *Cato* are from this edition, but I have Romanized proper names to avoid misleading stress.

6. Peter Smithers, *The Life of Joseph Addison,* 2d ed. (Oxford: Clarendon Press, 1968), pp. 261–64; hereafter cited in the text as Smithers.

7. *Remarks upon Cato* (1713) and *Letters upon the Sentiments . . .* (1721), in *The Critical Works of John Dennis,* ed. Edward Niles Hooker (Baltimore: John Hopkins Press, 1943), 2:41–80, 81–102.

sentation of natural affections, or of any state probable or possible in human life." The characters, he went on, "are made the vehicles of such sentiments and such expression that there is scarce a scene in the play which the reader does not wish to impress upon his memory."[8]

Chief among these passages was a collection of set pieces on patriotic virtue. In fact this play *was* the thing with which to catch the conscience of a king. Early in 1749, more than thirty-five years after its first production, *Cato* was performed at Leicester House by the children of the Prince of Wales. The future George III took the part of Cato's son Portius, and the future Lord North was the villainous Syphax. Prince George recited a special prologue for the occasion, confirming liberty as a special British heritage; it was a chance for him, even at the age of ten, to glory in the name of Briton:

> Shou'd this superior to my years be thought,
> Know—'tis the first great lesson I was taught.
> What, though a boy, it may with pride be said,
> A boy, in *England* born, in *England* bred:
> Where freedom well becomes the earliest state,
> For there the love of liberty's innate.[9]

The young actors may have looked a little silly in their sententious attitudes, and the Prince of Wales and his courtiers may have arranged this production to vex old George II as much as to instruct his young grandson. But *Cato* was a vehicle of instruction, even so. Years later Horace Walpole remembered the genuine acting talent it brought out in one of the princesses.[10] And apparently Prince Frederick was seriously weighing his eldest son's political training at just this time. Within a few days, he wrote a political will and testament for young George to have if he came to the throne (as in fact he did) directly upon the death of his grandfather.[11]

If *Cato* reached so far in England, it reached still farther in America. It

---

8. Samuel Johnson, *Lives of the English Poets,* ed. George Birkbeck Hill (Oxford: Clarendon Press, 1905), 2:132–33.

9. *London Magazine* 18 (1749): 37.

10. Walpole to Horace Mann, September 13, 1759, in *Correspondence,* ed. W. S. Lewis, 48 vols. (New Haven: Yale University Press, 1937–83), 21:327.

11. Sir George Young, *Poor Fred: The People's Prince* (London: Oxford University Press, 1937), pp. 172–75.

appealed to the taste of the English-speaking but Latin-reading audiences of the eighteenth century; and classicism and an admiration for Roman virtue may have had even more influence in America than in England, since America had fewer indigenous cultural monuments to hold them in check. A people who organized as war veterans into a Society of the Cincinnati, who monumentalized Washington as the noblest Roman of them all in their statuary and formal orations, who built and dwelt in Palladian country seats, and who signed their political essays with names like Novanglus, Caesar, Publius, and Cassius—such a public was quite ready to hear *Cato* and its echoes of ancient republicanism. This play also enjoyed two particular advantages: it was well suited to the early theatrical ventures of the colonies, and it took on special political significance in the course of the century.

In London, where theaters were continuous and competitive, this play was one standard among many. But in America conditions were very different. There were no large theatrical establishments until the 1750s, when a few valiant touring companies began to play in such centers as New York, Philadelphia, Williamsburg, and Charleston. During a long season such a company might produce twenty or thirty full-length plays in one place. An avid playgoer like Washington might catch other performances in his travels. But for most places in the colonies, drama remained rare. Even in the principal cities, theaters stood idle for years at a time. Theatrical diversions also ran against the moral scruples of many communities. Official censorship or community pressure snuffed out many an attempt to put on an evening's entertainment, not only in New England but all along the seaboard.

Cato was admirably suited to these circumstances. It was well known, the work of a famous moralist, and a highly virtuous script in its own right. More than one sensible producer held it forth as the first offering to wary audiences. When a rare amateur production was forcibly canceled in Boston in 1760, it was *Cato* that was in preparation.[12] When the Murray-Kean Company began to develop a theater in Philadelphia—causing more than one Quaker to regret that anything of the kind was encouraged—it was

12. Hugh F. Rankin, *The Theater in Colonial America* (Chapel Hill: University of North Carolina Press, 1965), p. 93.

Cato on opening night.[13] When students at William and Mary College planned a play in 1751, and their professor of moral philosophy raged into the dormitory and pulled down the curtains, it was *Cato* they had in mind.[14] The play found its way into many other public productions, as well as private theatricals and school exercises.[15] It was also a poetic work worth reading as a closet drama where no theater or prospect of a theater was at hand.

As the colonies moved toward revolution, *Cato* also came to represent American feelings as few other works could have done. The colonists frequently thought of themselves as Englishmen in America. They knew what they stood for, but they might find themselves hard pressed to defend it against Great Britain. Liberty meant, or should have meant, a range of rights and traditions that shielded men and property from arbitrary power. But it was hard to be forced to explain that. It was easy to protest against particular offenses—Stamp Acts, high-handed customs enforcement, Redcoats firing on a crowd, further taxes imposed by Parliament. But it was awkward to be driven to explaining liberty to the British. For liberty was embedded in British law and custom as it was nowhere else in the modern world. To rise up against British institutions was to risk damaging tenuous political gains men had made through the long course of history. Yet at the same time many writers held that the ground of true liberty in a nation was austere personal virtue in its people. Prosperous eighteenth-century England often seemed a realm of vice, luxury, and decadence, especially when compared to the homespun simplicity of the colonies.[16]

The poetry of *Cato* spoke deeply to these conditions. Here was a work from an earlier time, proclaiming liberty in line after line. It spoke for austere personal virtue, from the period between the Glorious Revolution and the advent of strong prime ministers and of Parliaments "corrupted" by systematic patronage. To the simplest imagination it held up a striking image of Cato in his desert stronghold, standing firm against the

13. Frederick B. Tolles, "A Literary Quaker: John Smith of Burlington and Philadelphia," *Pennsylvania Magazine of History and Biography* 65 (1941): 329.

14. Leon G. Tyler, ed., "Diary of John Blair," *William and Mary Quarterly* 8 (1899): 15.

15. Fredric M. Litto, "Addison's *Cato* in the Colonies," *William and Mary Quarterly*, 3d ser., 23 (1966): 431–49; Rankin, pp. 140, 169.

16. For a more thorough discussion of colonial respect for British rights and liberties, see Bernard Bailyn, *The Ideological Origins of the American Revolution* (Cambridge, Mass.: Harvard University Press, 1967), pp. 77–93.

encroachments of tyranny. Its scenes translated the values of republican Rome into the stately language of modern Britain. And since the play had remained a standard, acted repeatedly on both sides of the Atlantic, it was a familiar, comforting proof of a heritage shared and supported by Englishmen everywhere.

Furthermore, the figure of Cato the patriot had been colored and amplified in another popular work. The *Cato's Letters* of John Trenchard and Thomas Gordon, frequently reprinted and imitated in colonial newspapers and pamphlets, had become thoroughly absorbed into the language of political debate. These papers, first written for London newspapers in the 1720s, took their name from Addison's hero and arose from the strong opposition to the political corruption of their time. Before Britain and the colonies came into conflict, they had provided an entire generation with clear, readable arguments against arbitrary government. As Bernard Bailyn has put it in his study of pamphlet ideology in the revolutionary years, "The career of the half-mythological Roman and the words of the two London journalists merged indistinguishably" into "what might be called a 'Catonic' image, central to the political theory of the time."[17]

For all these reasons, *Cato* had become fixed in the memories of many colonists. Leading figures in the Revolution showed that they knew bits of Addison by heart. One example is Nathan Hale's regret that he had but one life to give for his country. This famous dying speech may well have been misreported. Hale had been teaching *Cato* before he took up arms, and his last words may have been "What pity is it / That we can die but once to serve our country!" (4.4.81–82).[18]

Patrick Henry's most famous speech also had a familiar ring to the educated Virginia audience that heard it in stunned silence. It is impossible to say whether Henry himself was thinking of Addison (he might have recalled passages from act 2, where Sempronius and Cato make impassioned pleas for war). And it is likely that a later reporter penned his famous concluding passage: "Give me liberty or give me death!"[19] But in

17. Bailyn, p. 44

18. George Dudley Seymour, *Documentary Life of Nathan Hale* (New Haven: privately printed, 1941), pp. 85–87, 376–82. What Nathan Hale actually said is still a matter of controversy; see three letters to *William and Mary Quarterly,* 3d ser., 43 (1986): 327–30.

19. Litto, p. 445; Stephen Taylor Olsen, "A Study in Disputed Authorship: The 'Liberty or Death' Speech" (Ph.D. diss., Pennsylvania State University, 1976).

any case the speech was highly dramatic, and St. George Tucker's account of it insists on the proper imagery: "Imagine to yourself this speech delivered with all the calm dignity of Cato of Utica; imagine to yourself the Roman Senate assembled in the capital when it was entered by the profane Gauls. . . . Imagine that you had heard that Cato addressing such a Senate." John Roane, another witness who added vivid details, says that after the word *liberty* the orator "stood like a Roman Senator defying Caesar, while the unconquerable spirit of Cato of Utica flashed from every feature," and then "closed the grand appeal with the solemn words 'or give me death!' "[20] Even if these later accounts are fabrications that have become legend replacing history, they reveal nevertheless how contemporaries wanted to see a Cato at the heart of the Revolution.

Even Benedict Arnold quoted this work. I suspect that he was trying to ingratiate himself with Major André by including an appropriate line from the theater in one of his first letters to that dashing special agent. "I cannot promise Success; I will deserve it," he wrote.[21] In the play, Cato's son Portius boasts to the secret traitor Sempronius: " 'Tis not in mortals to Command success, / But we'll do more, Sempronius; we'll Deserve it" (1.2.44–45).

It was George Washington, however, who absorbed *Cato* most deeply. In his youth he tried to model verses of his own upon lines from the play, and its heroic idealism echoes through many of his letters from the war years.[22] More impressive still is the fact that he sometimes reached out for lines from the play to describe difficult decisions he was making.

When Washington became engaged to Martha Custis in 1758, he was still in love with Sally Cary Fairfax, the brilliant young wife of his neighbor and patron, George William Fairfax of Belvoir. The chief evidence lies in two letters Washington wrote to Mrs. Fairfax while he was on duty that year in the French and Indian Wars. In both of them he made his love as clear as he could in discreet phrases that might be read by others. And in both of them he alluded to *Cato* as a way of simultaneously revealing and

20. William Wirt Henry, *Patrick Henry: Life, Correspondence, and Speeches* (New York, 1891), 1:264–65, 270.

21. Arnold to André, May 23, 1779, in Carl Van Doren, *Secret History of the American Revolution* (New York: Viking, 1941), p. 442.

22. John C. Fitzpatrick, *George Washington Himself* (Indianapolis: Bobbs-Merrill, 1933), p. 43; Paul Leicester Ford, *Washington and the Theatre,* Dunlap Society Publication, n.s. 8 (New York, 1899), p. 1.

concealing what he felt. The first letter, written from Fort Cumberland on September 12, contains two full paragraphs describing his perplexity as a "votary of love" for a woman he cannot name.[23] He does name Mrs. Curtis in his letter, but with stilted ambiguity; and he goes on to assert that his love is and must be secret, and that honor and his country's welfare should engage his thoughts instead. The editor of Washington's writings, John C. Fitzpatrick, has detected a teasing reference to *Cato* in these hints and maneuvers.[24] In the play, the Numidian leader Juba would marry Cato's daughter, but he cannot state his love or have any hope of it while Utica is besieged, as Portius makes clear:

> He loves our sister Marcia, greatly loves her,
> His eyes, his looks, his actions all betray it:
> But still the smother'd fondness burns within him.
> When most it swells, and labours for a vent,
> The sense of honour and desire of fame
> Drive the big passion back into his heart.

(1.1.83–88)

Washington seems to see a parallel dramatic situation in his own case. Ostensibly he claims that as a good soldier he should set aside thoughts of love—for Martha Custis or any other. But at the same time he confides his passion to Sally Fairfax and deftly suggests that a subordinate Juba can never hope to open such matters to the lady's superior kinsman—in this case, Mrs. Fairfax's good husband. The next letter (September 25) makes this interpretation explicit. "Do we still misunderstand the true meaning of each other's Letters?" Washington begins. "I think it must appear so, tho' I would feign hope the contrary as I cannot speak plainer without, But I'll say no more and leave you to guess the rest" (*Writings*, 2:292). He shifts the subject to the actions and losses of his regiment and to his despair of much success on his current expedition. But then comes a sudden return to restrained but direct compliment: "I should think my time more agreable spent believe me, in playing a part in Cato, with the Company you mention, and myself doubly happy in being the Juba to such a Marcia, as you must make" (*Writings*, 2:293).

23. Washington, *Writings*, 2:287. This letter was auctioned and lost from view in 1877 and its authenticity has been doubted. It is now in the Houghton Library at Harvard.
24. Fitzpatrick, *George Washington Himself*, p. 111.

The cruel winter at Valley Forge forced Washington to recall another detail from the play. One of its famous set pieces is a speech at the end of act 4, in which Cato urges his son to retreat from Caesar's power to a life of rural detachment. It concludes with the familiar quotation: "When vice prevails, and impious men bear sway, / The post of honour is a private station" (4.4.141–42). Buffeted from many quarters by suggestions that Gates or Lee might make a better commander, Washington for a moment considered resigning and going home to Mount Vernon. He expressed himself plainly to a correspondent:

> Neither interested nor ambitious views led me into the service, I did not solicit the command, but accepted it after much entreaty, with all that diffidence which a conscious want of ability and experience equal to the discharge of so important a trust, must naturally create in a mind not quite devoid of thought; and after I did engage, pursued the great line of my duty, and the object in view (as far as my judgment could direct) as pointedly as the needle to the pole. So soon then as the public gets dissatisfied with my services, or a person is found better qualified to answer her expectation, I shall quit the helm with as much satisfaction, and retire to a private station with as much content, as ever the wearied pilgrim felt upon his safe arrival in the Holy-land, or haven of hope; and shall wish most devoutly, that those who come after may meet with more prosperous gales than I have done, and less difficulty.[25]

"Private station" is not just a coincidental phrase here; when Washington was about to leave the presidency he again wrote letters about his "ultimate determination 'To seek the Post of Honor in a private Station.' "[26]

At around this time the idea of Washington as an American Cato was taking other forms. For a 1778 performance in New Hampshire, Jonathan M. Sewall wrote an epilogue to the play, in which the identification was at last explicit and public:

25. To Rev. William Gordon, January 23, 1778, *Writings*, 10:338. On February 15, Washington assured Gordon that he had no intention of resigning, unless it were the will of the public, not of a "faction" (*Writings*, 10:462–63). The long passage quoted here nonetheless records Washington in a wintry mood. It also reveals his deep strengths. "Let those who subscribe to the canard that Washington could not write well read this paragraph a second time" (James Thomas Flexner, *George Washington in the American Revolution (1775–1783)* [Boston: Little, Brown, 1968], p. 266).

26. To David Humphreys, June 12, 1796, and to Alexander Hamilton, June 26, 1796, *Writings*, 35:92, 103.

Did Rome's brave senate nobly strive t'oppose
The mighty torrent of domestic foes?
And boldly arm the virtuous few, and dare
The desp'rate perils of unequal war?
    Our senate too, the same bold deed has done,
And for a CATO, arm'd a WASHINGTON![27]

And at the 1778 performance at Valley Forge, Washington and Addison's
hero actually faced one another.

No such play could have been imagined in the winter. There could hardly
be a theater where men had to build rude huts for their shelter, or costumes
where there was a desperate lack of uniforms and shoes. Even if there had
been such material resources, entertainments like plays were officially for-
bidden. In 1774 the Continental Congress had passed (and Washington,
who was then a member, had signed) an "association" against "gaming,
cock fighting, exhibitions of shews, plays, and other expensive diversions";
thereafter all theatrical activity in the colonies had ceased.[28] It ceased, that is,
except in areas occupied by the British. The contrast was stark. No sooner
did General Howe move into Philadelphia than advertisements appeared
for a copyist, an account clerk, and carpenters—all "wanted for the
Play-house."[29] Between January and May, the new company put on thirteen
plays, not counting the elaborate pageant called the *Mischianza,* which Major
André staged at enormous cost just before Howe sailed for England and
Philadelphia was evacuated.[30]

The more chaste performance of *Cato* is described in only one surviving
account, a letter a few days later by William Bradford, Jr. He was a son of
the Philadelphia family that had long rivaled Franklin as printers. A
correspondent of his Princeton classmate James Madison, he would one
day be attorney general in Washington's cabinet. Both he and his father

27. Jonathan M. Sewall, *Miscellaneous Poems* (Portsmouth, N.H., 1801), p. 108. This Jonathan
Sewall was a cousin of the lawyer whom we saw opposed to John Adams in chapter 3. He went on to
write hundreds of lines in praise of Washington, including a complete versification of the Farewell
Address.

28. Ford, pp. 24–25.

29. *Pennsylvania Ledger,* December 31, 1777, cited in Thomas Clark Pollock, *The Philadelphia
Theatre in the Eighteenth Century* (Philadelpha: University of Pennsylvania Press, 1933), p. 34.

30. The costs and splendor of this event are recounted in detail in James Thomas Flexner, *The
Traitor and the Spy: Benedict Arnold and John André* (New York: Harcourt, Brace, 1953), pp. 308–15.

served in the war, and at Valley Forge he held the rank of lieutenant colonel—a gentleman-officer at the age of twenty-three. On May 14 he wrote to his young sister Rachel, who was in Trenton, and teasingly invited her to extend her jaunt:

> The Camp could now afford you some entertainment. The manouvering of the Army is in itself a sight that would Charm you.—Besides these, the Theatre is opened—Last Monday Cato was performed before a very numerous and splendid audience. His Excellency and Lady, Lord Stirling, the Countess and Lady Kitty, and Mrs. Green were part of the Assembly. The scenery was in Taste—and the performance admirable—Colonel George did his part to Admiration—he made an excellent *die* (as they say)—Pray heaven, he don't *die* in earnest—for yesterday he was seized with the pleurisy and lies extremely ill—If the Enemy does not retire from Philadelphia soon, our Theatrical amusements will continue—The fair Penitent with the Padlock will soon be acted. The "recruiting Officer" is also on foot.
>
> I hope however we shall be disappointed in all these by the more agreeable Entertainment of taking possession of Philadelphia—There are strong rumors that the English are meditating a retreat—Heaven send it—for I fear we shall not be able to force them to go these two months.[31]

This description suggests that *Cato* may have been the only play there was time for. Washington saw it, along with General Stirling, his wife and daughter, and the wife of General Greene. "Colonel George" was a friend of the Bradfords; he is mentioned as a scapegrace young man in later notes.[32] Here he must have had a principal role, Cato or Cato's son Marcus, if he died on stage. The other plays mentioned—Nicholas Rowe's *The Fair Penitent* (1703), George Farquhar's *The Recruiting Officer* (1706), and Isaac Bickerstaffe's *The Padlock* (1768)—were also popular works, though far less edifying. But as Bradford surmised, the British were about to leave Philadelphia, beginning on May 16. On the twentieth he again

31. Historical Society of Pennsylvania, Wallace Papers (Bradford), 1:58; I have expanded abbreviations. A slightly inaccurate version is printed with other Bradford letters of this period in *Pennsylvania Magazine of History and Biography* 40 (1916): 335–43.

32. Wallace Papers (Bradford), 1:63, 69, 71.

wrote his sister: "I no longer invite you here—all is hurry and bustle—our plays and other amusements seem to be laid aside and everyone is preparing for a sudden movement."[33]

No one seems to have recorded further hard evidence about this play, or specifically remembered it later. It is impossible to know how elaborately it was done, or even how much of the play was actually recited. But what we have seen of the play, its history, and its associations supports some conclusions about what it must have meant in this setting. On the one hand, we have a telling clue to an identity Washington may have associated with himself. On the other, we have a performance that carried the possibilities in Addison's play about as far as they could go.

The play must have reminded its audience of Washington as its lines stressed the virtues of Cato and its scenes recalled analogous strains in his generalship. Perhaps this was the effect intended by the players, especially if they were his officers. It is tempting to think that they meant the production as a compliment to their general, a return for his reception for officers at the feu de joye. That Washington did attend to play and that it called attention to his own character is certain. We can only surmise how he responded.

He might have been uncomfortable with such attention. He liked plays, but not public adulation. In New York in 1789 it was known that the new president was particularly mentioned in *Darby's Return*. Washington attended the play, and its author wrote that the audience watched his expressions closely. When one character asked another how Washington looked at the inauguration, the president was visibly embarrassed. When Darby answered that he had not seen him "because he had mistaken a man 'all in lace and glitter, botherum and shine' for him," Washington "indulged in that which was with him extremely rare, a hearty laugh."[34]

But he may have reacted differently at Valley Forge. The rather large and splendid audience would have comprised his comrades-in-arms, and the virtues of the play would have reflected well on all them. Some lines must have called attention to the commander in chief:

33. Wallace Papers (Bradford), 1:59.
34. William Dunlap, *History of the American Theatre*, 2d ed. (1833; rpt. New York: Burt Franklin, 1963), 1:160–61. Washington certainly was capable of laughing and of turning a comic remark with good effect. He "had a great deal of that dry humour which he knew how to make use of on proper occasions," as Du Ponceau records with examples (Du Ponceau, p. 211).

> Turn up they eyes to Cato!
> There may'st thou see to what a godlike height
> The Roman virtues lift up mortal man.
> While good, and just, and anxious for his friends,
> He's still severely bent against himself;
> Renouncing sleep, and rest, and food, and ease,
> He strives with thirst and hunger, toil and heat;
> And when his fortune sets before him all
> The pomps and pleasures that his soul can wish,
> His rigid virtue will accept of none.
>
> (1.4.49–58)

But others gave expression to a more general idealism that applied to all the forces and the new nation they were creating. And some lines resembled words that had actually passed between Washington and his men. Every great commander rouses his men by appealing to the virtues of their common cause; Washington became eloquent about sacrifice in the name of liberty. As late as March 1, his general orders contained passages that castigated unmanly murmuring against hardships and extolled the transcendent prize that would crown American soldiery: "the Admiration of the World, the Love of their Country and the Gratitude of Posterity!" (*Writings,* 11:10). Now the men who had heard and read such exhortations through several months, who had suffered, buried others, and prepared again for war, could hear the same tone in the speech with which Cato stifles a mutiny:

> Remember, O my friends, the laws, the rights,
> The generous plan of power deliver'd down,
> From age to age, by your renown'd Fore-fathers,
> (So dearly bought, the price of so much blood)
> O never let it perish in your hands!
> But piously transmit it to your children.
> Do thou, great Liberty, inspire our souls,
> And make our lives in thy possession happy,
> Or our deaths glorious in thy just defence.
>
> (3.5.73–81)

Finally, it was Washington's prerogative to approve the staging of any play, let alone honor this one by his presence. Because of his own familiarity with *Cato,* he must have known how it would affect this audience. And it is pertinent to recall that at the end of the feu de joye a few days earlier he had allowed himself to be cheered. "When the General took his leave," an officer wrote, "there was a universal clap, with loud huzzas, which continued till he had proceeded a quarter of a mile, during which time there were a thousand hats tossed in the air. His Excellency turned around with his retinue, and huzzaed several times."[35] Now he may have been eager to raise his own and his men's morale; *Cato* would provide the ritual of their high fellowship.

If so, this play provides a clue to the life of this remarkable American. Our image of Washington may never be completely free of our sense of him as a hero fixed at the center of a tableau or a series of tableaux—including four of Trumbull's eight great Revolutionary panels. But here at least the backdrop fits him closely, has depth, and reflects the contours of his mind as well as that of his large frame. Here he is not the equestrian general or the Virginia aristocrat or the national patriarch. Instead, Cato of Utica stands as his counterpart. Cato is awesome, to be sure: a paragon of stern self-discipline in the name of a great cause. But he is barely able to carry a unique burden—the civilian patriot turned temporary general, holding together a composite army against overwhelming odds. Washington emerges more lifelike than this figure. He attended the play, shared the applause, and then went on with his tedious duties.

Conversely, this performance provides the final measure of Addison's drama. From the first, *Cato* was a play that audiences saw *through.* The playwright himself focused on a noble character from history. The Whigs and Tories of 1713 had seen Marlborough and Bolingbroke. The circle at Leicester House had seen Prince George as Portius and Portius as Prince George. And when topical references subsided, the mind could turn to the author. "We pronounce the name of Cato, but we think on Addison," wrote Dr. Johnson with the admiration of a fellow moralist.[36] When

35. *The Writings of George Washington,* ed. Jared Sparks, 12 vols. (Boston, 1834–37), 5:356–57.

36. *Johnson on Shakespeare,* ed. Arthur Sherbo, Yale Edition of the Works of Samuel Johnson (New Haven: Yale University Press, 1968), 7:84.

Alexander Pope attacked Addison in the *Epistle to Dr. Arbuthnot,* he cut deep by describing the foppish, perverted hero of a "little Senate." Earlier, when Pope had read the play in manuscript, he had seen through it to a different image. If it ever came on stage, he wrote, "we shall enjoy that which Plato thought the greatest pleasure an exalted soul could be capable of, a view of virtue itself great in person, colour, and action."[37]

All these visions of the play, however, shared a common failing. Each object they fixed upon was much greater or much smaller than the substance of the play, even taking into account its glaring pomposities. Cato of Utica was manifestly grander than any modern politician, essayist, or prince; and yet he was stiffly virtuous at best.

But at Valley Forge the audience was prepared to see this hero with an even admiration. They might face the stage, see through its artifice, and yet feel no impossible disparity between the characters and themselves. Washington was all that Cato had been—as unbending in his virtues and as heroic in his stature among Americans. His followers had another advantage, too. Addison's hero represented virtue perishing. Cato died on his sword, rendered all but powerless by tyranny.

> These are thy triumphs, thy exploits, O Caesar!
> Now is Rome fall'n indeed!

> (5.4.78–79)

In 1778 Washington and his armies were imagining not defeat or suicide but a new ascent of virtue in a victorious, independent America. The celebrations at camp may have ended with this play, but the men prepared to march on—back into Philadelphia and across New Jersey in pursuit of Redcoats—with new and well-justified strengths.

37. *The Correspondence of Alexander Pope,* ed. George Sherburn (Oxford: Clarendon Press, 1956), 1:173. Pope wrote the prologue for the first performance of *Cato* in 1713.

A Valediction Forbidding Mourning

Like most relics of Washington, his Farewell Address is more striking as a symbol than as a means of transmitting the ideas of a living man. It is rightly remembered as a gesture of renunciation; with these words the first president gracefully relinquished power and opened the way for its smooth transfer to a new administration. The address was also an instrument of and monument to early American policy; it expressed the new nation's resolve to stay free of involvement in European wars and to turn the efforts of government toward developing strength on this continent.[1] But another aspect of the address is equally important. In composing it, Washington did not work alone. He asked for preliminary drafts from James Madison and Alexander Hamilton and incorporated their work into the final version, which he sent out for carefully timed newspaper publication. By asking these particular men to help with this great address, Washington called again on well-tried younger allies. He also closed off their long association as three closely bound public personalities.

Washington, Hamilton, and Madison had already come together twice before in the newspapers of the day, to explain or reinforce the strengths of

1. The monumental character of the address is admirably surveyed in Arthur A. Markovitz, "Washington's Farewell Address and the Historians: A Critical Review," *Pennsylvania Magazine of History and Biography* 94 (1970): 173–91.

the new Constitution. In 1787 Hamilton and Madison had collaborated on the *Federalist* papers, defending the Constitution and urging its adoption by the several states. Although they were nor directly allied with Washington in these papers, they stayed in touch with him as they wrote. They certainly bore in mind that Washington had chaired their deliberations in the Philadelphia convention and that the new document had his endorsement and the promise of his continuing leadership in the struggle for its adoption. A few years later, in 1793, Hamilton and Madison again took up their pens in newspaper series, but this time as adversaries. The occasion was Washington's brief proclamation of neutrality toward both Britain and France. Hamilton as "Pacificus" defended this proclamation as a wise move and a proper exercise of executive power. Madison as "Helvidius" denied that it was wise and publicly questioned its constitutionality.

By pulling together the two men's talents and reorganizing their contributions in his own handwriting, Washington made the Farewell Address a balanced summary of his presidency and its accomplishments. He might have given his collaborators the notion that they were writing this document, that they were supplying the president with his last public words, and that thus they were the scriptwriters for his exit from the public stage. To later readers, Washington may still give the impression that he leaned on Hamilton and Madison for essential support. But it is also possible that Washington here, as throughout his administration, had a keen sense of how to manage other men's energies and draw them out for the larger good of their country.

Washington's perplexities about leaving office weighed heavily on his mind in 1792, the last year of his first term as president. In May he wrote to James Madison from Mount Vernon, recalling their confidential conversations on this subject and proposing a formal address. A central paragraph of that letter outlining what Washington had in mind must be quoted in full:

> I would fain carry my request to you farther than is asked above, although I am sensible that your compliance with it must add to your trouble; but as the recess may afford you leizure, and I flatter myself you have dispositions to oblige me, I will, without apology desire (if

the measure in itself should strike you as proper, & likely to produce public good, or private honor) that you would turn your thoughts to a valadictory address from me to the public; expressing in plain & modest terms:—that having been honored with the Presidential Chair, and to the best of my abilities contributed to the organization & administration of the government.—that having arrived at a period of life when the private walks of it, in the shade of retirement, becomes necessary, and will be most pleasing to me;—and the spirit of the government may render a rotation in the Elective officers of it more congenial with their ideas of liberty & safety, that I take my leave of them as a public man;—and in bidding them adieu (retaining no other concern than such as will arise from fervent wishes for the prosperity of my Country) I take the liberty at my departure from civil, as I formerly did at my military exit, to invoke a continuation of the blessings of Providence upon it—and upon all those who are the supporters of its interests, and the promoters of harmony, order & good government.[2]

On a first reading this may seem a pompous tangle of intentions and hesitations. Despite some vagaries of punctuation, the paragraph consists of only one long meandering sentence and a modern reader may need to pare it down in order to grasp it at all: "I want you to write a Farewell from me to the public; explain that since the government is now well established and I have grown old I will retire from the presidency and take my leave with every good wish for the country." But to a reader who, like Madison, is familiar with Washington's style or who will reread the paragraph a few times, it unfolds as the expression of an extraordinary being. Every phrase has been carefully considered, settled upon, and ordered in constructing a suitable pattern for his farewell. Earlier in this letter, Washington has told Madison that he has again and again "revolved" the problems of his retirement "with thoughtful anxiety." This sentence contains a dozen delicate considerations masterfully compressed into a formal and coherent—though not yet conclusive—plan of action.

2. Washington to Madison, May 20, 1792, in *Washington's Farewell Address*, ed. Victor Hugo Paltsits (New York: New York Public Library, 1935), p. 222; hereafter cited as Paltsits. A rough draft of this letter is also given on p. 219.

To hold these ideas together, Washington writes with an instinctive sense of balance. He relates one phrase to another that resembles it grammatically, but differs in emphasis or meaning. He will add to Madison's trouble, but he knows Madison has the leisure and the desire for this task. He hopes the address may "produce public good, or private honor." He sees that the time is ripe in terms of both the public welfare and his personal comfort. This civil retirement may recall his "military exit." He will invoke blessings on the country and also on its most selfless supporters. Some of these balances may seem merely habitual, the commonplace flourishes of an eighteenth-century pen. But with them, Washington is also weighing himself before and after the act of retiring. "I take my leave of them as a public man" is counterposed to "bidding them adieu" as a disinterested private citizen. The address is to be a significant deed of the president, but it is also to carry the voice of a man apart from his office; it is to recall the former general and also to evoke some sympathy for the enduring Virginia planter, in his "private Walks . . . in the shade of retirement."

Thus Washington holds in one hand the meaning of his life and in the other the meaning of his death. This is a point that he covers with euphemism and that no one around him could directly mention. His sixtieth birthday occurred in February 1792, and it was then that he began approaching confidential advisers about the best means of leaving office. There is no record of what he said to Madison on February 19, but he spoke to Jefferson ten days later about his failing health. He said "that he really felt himself growing old, his bodily health less firm, his memory, always bad, becoming worse, and perhaps the other faculties of his mind showing a decay to others of which he was insensible himself, that his apprehension particularly oppressed him, that he found morever [sic] his activity lessened, business therefore more irksome, and tranquility & retirement become an irresistible passion."[3] When he spoke to Madison early in May, he again stressed "that he found himself also in the decline of life, his health becoming sensibly more infirm, & perhaps his faculties also; that the fatigues & disagreeableness of his situation were in fact scarcely tolerable to him."[4] For reasons of his private comfort and those of

3. Jefferson's *Anas* for February 29, 1792, in *The Writings of Thomas Jefferson*, ed. Paul Leicester Ford, 10 vols. (New York, 1892–98), 1:175.
4. Madison's Personal Memoranda, in Paltsits, p. 214.

state, Washington disliked the thought of dying in office. He did not want to be remembered as someone who had given up his military command only to return and hold supreme power to the end of his days. He was also highly conscious, from his first days as president, that every gesture could become a precedent binding upon his successors. He wanted to avoid any suggestion that the presidency should be held until death. As he says in his instructions to Madison: "the spirit of the government may render a rotation in the Elective officers of it more congenial with their [the people's] ideas of liberty & safety." He refrains from saying that no one should continue to hold office indefinitely, only that rotation is fitting under the Constitution; his own retirement, then, in apparent health would be the proper conclusion to his tenure as the first president.

The notion of retirement before death gives special power to this paragraph and to the address that grew out of it. From phrase to phrase, Washington alternates between stiff formality and an ingratiating admission of his personal vulnerability. He commands Madison, yet pleads for his aid. He begins courteously, yet presses on with urgency. Washington was always reserved with his associates. He addressed them with an oxymoron—"my dear Sir"—that could be taken as a conventional courtesy, as an avowal of affectionate feeling, or as a reminder of official respect. Here that ambiguity plays across every idea. Madison should consider what is best, yet must do exactly what he is told. He is drawn into the intimacy of a personal secret, yet held at arm's length by a carefully drafted letter of instruction. Washington, although contemplating a magnanimous gesture of resignation, feels compelled to it by his increasing frailty and discomfort in office. But he is uncertain about how to proceed.

His first instruction is that this address should go out to the public "in plain & modest terms." The president had singled Madison out earlier in the month for a private conversation on the mode and time of an address. Washington had put forward the idea of addressing Congress, but hesitated out of fear of becoming entangled in congressional replies and further explanations. A few days later Madison reported that he had hit upon no other plan, though he agreed that the idea of addressing Congress was vulnerable to weighty objections (Paltsits, pp. 213, 217). Now Washington tells Madison he has decided to address the people directly, which in 1792 meant through publication in the newspapers. But he is still wavering about the timing and tone of such a message. "In revolving this subject myself," he says earlier in this letter, "my judgment has always been embarrassed." To make an early announcement might seem a pompous maneuver, risking either the appearance of self-importance or the charge of angling for renomination. Yet to keep silent would imply consent and make it more difficult for him to decline later on.

Furthermore, Washington was chary of engaging in public controversy through the press. Much of his discomfort in the presidency was due to newspaper attacks upon his administration's policies. He could not have been more comfortable with the prospect of retiring through this medium than through addressing Congress.

It was no secret to him that the tension in his cabinet between Hamilton and Jefferson was being amplified in public by Philadelphia newspapers the two men were helping to support. The *Gazette of the United States,* edited by John Fenno, was subsidized in part by printing contracts from the Treasury Department and was glowing in its praises of the government, particularly Hamilton's measures. To counter this, Jefferson offered Philip Freneau a sinecure clerkship in the State Department, which drew him to Philadelphia where he established the *National Gazette* in 1791. This journal relentlessly hounded Hamilton and praised Jefferson. At the same time that Washington was planning his retirement, this simmering newspaper war was erupting into overt accusations and counterblasts between the two sides, revealing a deep rift in the cabinet to anyone who could read.[5] In July Washington told Jefferson how deeply these battles offended him. He complained that "the pieces lately published, & particularly in Freneau's paper seemed to have in view the exciting opposition to the govmt. . . . He considered those papers as attacking him directly, for he must be a fool indeed to swallow the little sugar plumbs here & there thrown out to him. That in condemning the admn of the govmt they condemned him, for if they thought there were measures pursued contrary to his sentiment, they must conceive him too careless to attend to them or too stupid to understand them."[6]

Careless and stupid Washington was not. Thus, his calling upon Madi-

5. See John C. Miller, *The Federalist Era, 1789–1801* (New York: Harper & Row, 1960), pp. 89–92, for a standard account of these newspaper wars.
6. *Anas* for July 20, 1792, in Jefferson, *Writings,* 1:199.

son may well have been a sensible means of protecting himself. By implicating one of Jefferson's allies in this address in defense of his character and actions, he might find a middle course, avoiding editorial attack from either side.

Still, Washington was firm about putting his own imprint on his message. It was not to be merely a resignation, with a tidy explanation of his reasons for accepting office and now yielding it. It was to be a valedictory, a final leave-taking meant to recall and seal his earlier resignation as commander in chief.

That message of 1783, in the form of a circular letter to the state governors, was another occasion Washington had seized for conveying his ideals of American government. He had called then for support for the union of the states, even though the war was over and the armies were on the point of disbanding. He had urged the potential greatness of the new nation and then listed four measures essential to continued independence: indissoluble union, just payment of public debts, continuance of a military establishment, and suppression of local and sectional rivalries. After discussing these at length—motivated, as he said, by a strong sense of both public duty and personal concern—he concluded with an "earnest prayer" that God would bless each state and incline the hearts of all men to charity, humility, and peace.[7] Known as "Washington's Legacy," this long message had been cherished as a summing up of what the war had meant and what America might become.[8] It was a document that Washington did not want tarnished or eclipsed. In recalling it to Madison's attention, he is plainly asking him to amplify and renew it in the memories of his countrymen. His further instructions to Madison, concerning the unique prospects of a strong and free America, argue that the new address should reinforce the message of the Legacy, making it an even more powerful blessing and prayer.

Madison's reply and his draft of the address show that all these concerns were noted and borne in mind. Madison answered each main point Washington had raised and again weighed all the alternatives. He agreed that

7. *The Writings of George Washington*, ed. John C. Fitzpatrick, 39 vols. (Washington, D. C.: U.S. Government Printing Office, 1933–44), 26:483–96.
8. Douglas Southall Freeman, *George Washington*, 7 vols. (New York: Scribners, 1948–57), 5:446.

the message should be "a direct address to the people who are your only constituents" and that it should be made through the newspapers. There was now no opportunity for addressing Congress or for writing to the state governments as in "the former valedictory address." Madison considered that a full valedictory address should coincide with the announcement that Washington would not run again and urged publication around the middle of September. "The precedent at your military exit, might also subject an omission now to conjectures and interpretations, which it would not be well to leave room for." In the end, Madison wrote a draft that could be adapted for delivery in September or on a later occasion, and he stuck close to Washington's instructions. "You will readily observe that in executing it I have aimed at that plainness & modesty of language which you had in view, and which indeed are so peculiarly becoming the character and the occasion; and that I have had little more to do, as to the matter, than to follow the just and comprehensive outline which you had sketched."[9]

Madison's brief manuscript actually depends on Washington's key phrases. In it, the president claims "that I have contributed towards the organization and administration of the Government the best exertions of which a very fallible judgment was capable"; he admits that "private walks . . . in the shade of retirement" are "as necessary as they will be acceptable to me"; and he points out that rotation in high office "may equally accord with the republican spirit of our constitution, and the ideas of liberty and safety entertained by the people" (Paltsits, pp. 160–61). The entire draft closely follows the sentiments and phrasing of Washington's letter to Madison. Madison may have reread the Legacy address of 1783 and slightly altered some lines to recall Washington's earlier words. He also toned down the idea of invoking the blessings of God. In his draft, it is incorporated in a paragraph on Washington's "vows which I shall carry with me to my retirement and my grave, that Heaven may continue to favor the people of the United States with the choicest tokens of its beneficence." The draft ends with Washington's modest "wishes and hopes" and "extreme solicitude" for American liberty, prosperity, and happiness (Paltsits, pp. 161–63). As a whole Madison's collaboration

9. Madison to Washington, June 20, 1792, in Paltsits, pp. 227–29.

does not extend much further than expanding, smoothing, and reconfirming the ideas that Washington already had settled on.

Madison's draft, however, came to Washington accompanied by further protests that the president should continue in office for another term. Madison had already bluntly explained that none of the likely successors—Adams, Jefferson, or Jay—would fill the office nearly as well.[10] Jefferson had confided that he intended to leave public life when Washington did; he also reasoned that Washington could retire with dignity before a second term ran its course.[11] Hamilton, Robert Morris, and Edmund Randolph registered their sense that Washington was still indispensable to the establishment of a stable government (Paltsits, pp. 229–35). September came and went, Washington made no declaration of retirement, and he was reelected unanimously in December.

He again began to plan a formal statement of his retirement in 1796, the last year of his second term. By May he had taken out Madison's draft, pondered it again, and prepared a new introduction and a long new section covering his second administration. He wrote out a new draft of all these materials in his own hand and then approached a new collaborator. He wrote to Alexander Hamilton on May 15, enclosing this draft and asking for his help in revising it to make it as perfect as possible.

At this point, Washington's strategy was firmly decided. This would be an address to the people, in a plain style, to be published in the newspapers. It was also to appear shortly before the election so that the present administration would enjoy full power and authority to the last possible moment.

But Washington's second term had been troubled. By 1796 he could not take his farewell as comfortably or graciously as he might have done in 1792. Allies who had then worked together under his authority had now fallen out with each other and left the government. Jefferson and Hamilton had never been reconciled; both had resigned. Other cabinet officers had left and been replaced. Washington had given his support to policies of the Federalists and found himself vilified by the Republican press. To his critics (and perhaps he agreed) he had stayed on too long; he was no longer the national hero entirely above party. In fact, when Congress

10. Madison's Personal Memoranda, in Paltsits, p. 216.
11. Jefferson to Washington, May 23, 1792, in Paltsits, p. 225.

voted him a final expression of gratitude, it fell into a nasty wrangle about whether he had provided wise and virtuous leadership![12]

With an eye to these troubles, Washington recast his message in a defensive mood. He explained to Hamilton that he included Madison's draft on purpose, as proof that he had intended to resign years earlier. "And besides, it may contribute to blunt, if it does not turn aside, some of the shafts which it may be presumed will be aimed at my annunciation of this event;—among which—conviction of fallen popularity, and despair of being re-elected, will be levelled at me with dexterity and keenness."[13] At the close of that draft, Washington now added an explanatory paragraph:

> Had the situation of our public affairs continued to wear the same aspect they assumed at the time the aforegoing address was drawn I should not have taken the liberty of troubling you—my fellow citizens—with any new sentiments or with a rep[et]ition, more in detail, of those which are therein contained; but considerable changes having taken place both at home & abroad, I shall ask your indulgence while I express with more lively sensibility, the following most ardent wishes of my heart. (Paltsits, p. 168)

What followed were nine sketchy paragraphs, all expressed as wishes: "That party disputes . . . may subside"; that we "not be . . . ungrateful to our Creator"; that we pay all our just debts; that we "avoid connecting ourselves with the Politics of any Nation, farther than shall be found necessary to regulate our own trade"; that every citizen cherish America above all other nations; that we remain ready for war, but do our best to build national strength in a long era of peace; that we suppress party disputes to a common commitment to neutrality; that "our Union may be as lasting as time"; and that government departments not encroach on one another. Then in four long paragraphs Washington took occasion to defend himself personally. Noting that the *Gazette of the United States* had libeled him and done everything possible to undermine his authority, he recalled his long sacrifices to the country, his struggles to do his best in hard new duties, and his avoidance of all personal gain (Paltsits, pp. 168–73).

12. Freeman, 7:422 and notes.
13. Washington to Hamilton, May 15, 1796, in Paltsits, p. 242.

As Washington sensed, this longer draft had its problems. It repeated many ideas, merely hinted at some points, and came dangerously close to stridency and anger. The president sent it to Hamilton with an appeal for assistance. During years as his aide-de-camp, Hamilton had helped him draft his papers; in the government and out of it he had continued to prepare addresses and official messages. Even though Hamilton was now a private lawyer in New York, he was still being called upon to write substantial state papers.[14] Washington urged him to take this one in hand, to not only retouch it but completely rewrite it if necessary. In the latter case he wished to see two versions: Hamilton's complete draft and Washington's original draft with Hamilton's amendments and corrections.

Hamilton followed these instructions faithfully. He wrote both a complete new draft and an amended version that might be attached to the draft Madison had prepared and Washington had enlarged. (Paltsits has titled these, respectively, "Hamilton's Original Major Draft" and "Hamilton's Draft for Incorporating.") He relied in both versions on Washington's instructions and language, but he sorted out and regrouped clusters of ideas. He elaborated small points and turned Washington's strained "wishes" into reasoned, dignified exhortations on the strength of Union, the dangers of party, and the wisdom of political neutrality toward foreign powers. He thus muted Washington's personal defense by working it into the sturdy structure of a long and clear-sighted testament, consistent with the president's policies and accomplishments in two terms of office.

These revisions cost Hamilton several weeks of thoughtful labor. He put together an outline for his major draft and then wrote it out, revised it, went over it with John Jay, and finally sent it to Washington with the promise of soon completing the draft for incorporating. Eventually he sent that along, too. But Washington was persuaded that the major draft was clearly superior; he accepted it as the working draft, sent it back to Hamilton for some further touches, and then began to ask for advice on the best means of getting it into print (Paltsits, pp. 43–48).

By means of these revisions Washington and Hamilton effected important changes in the meaning and weight of the address. It was no longer an echo or reminder of the Legacy address of 1783. This was a grander

14. See Paltsits, pp. 25–28, for a review of major papers Hamilton wrote for Washington.

performance, designed to supplant that earlier farewell. The emphasis on "plain and modest terms" was abandoned in favor of a more dignified tone, "better calculated," Washington remarked, "to meet the eye of discerning readers" including foreign leaders.[15] Appeals to the blessings of Providence were replaced by recollections of shared accomplishments and injunctions to maintain a strong Constitution. And the division between Madison's version and the added remarks of Washington's draft was subtly transformed into a new reflection on the president's two terms in office. A stress on union and just internal policies was associated with the first term, but the address moved to its climax in summarizing the sound foreign policy that had been formulated and maintained over the last four years.

To a critical eye, then and now, the address could read as a well-calculated recapitulation of Federalist party policies. But this is true not because Hamilton took over and manipulated Washington's occasion for his own ends. It is rather that Washington's own view of himself had changed. Now he was not taking his leave as a general who had been called back to temporary, uncomfortable duty in a brief term as president. He had served as president for almost eight years—about the same amount of time he had served as commander in chief. In office longer than all the members of his cabinet, he had done more than anyone to shape the new government, and in doing so, had taken a full dose of abuse.

Finally, Washington carefully transformed Hamilton's draft into copy for the press. He corrected it, deleted some portions, inserted new ones, and weighed again phrases that had been evolving for more than four years. What went to the printer was a sheaf of papers in Washington's script, with further emendations in his hand. The opening paragraphs still took their shape from the version Madison had prepared, but the closing words were Washington's own. He picked up what Hamilton had made of his apology for unavoidable faults: "I shall also carry with me the hope that my Country will never cease to view them with indulgence; and that after forty five years of my life dedicated to its Service, with an upright zeal, the faults of incompetent abilities will be consigned to oblivion, as

15. Washington to Hamilton, August 25, 1796, in Paltsits, p. 252.

myself must soon be to the mansions of rest." Then he pressed on with another paragraph—developed out of Madison's draft, revised in Hamilton's, and deleted from an earlier section of this holograph.

> Relying on its kindness in this as in other things, and actuated by that fervent love towards it, which is so natural to a man, who views in it the native soil of himself and his progenitors for several Generations;—I anticipate with pleasing expectation that retreat, in which I promise myself to realize, without alloy, the sweet enjoyment of partaking, in the midst of my fellow citizens, the benign influence of good Laws under a free Government—the ever favourite object of my heart, and the happy reward, as I trust, of our mutual cares, labours and dangers.[16]

Thus all ends in tranquility and rest, borne up by kindness and indulgence. The prosperity and justice of America merge with one man's "native soil," his "mansions of rest," and the happy rewards for labors accomplished. Washington gracefully departs for an eternal Mount Vernon.

To complete this ritual the president also arranged an unchallengeable exit. When the address reached the public on September 19, he was in his coach traveling to Mount Vernon. He did not return to Philadelphia until the end of October, when the voting for his successor was about to take place.[17]

Washington thus displayed fine touches of mastery, not to say poetry, in composing this farewell. He initiated the message and completed it, retaining his control over the contributions of others. But because he tacitly incorporated some of Hamilton's and Madison's ideas, they, too, can be found in the Farewell Address.

Both men were about twenty years younger than Washington, but by 1792 both had already given long years to the development of the American government. At the outbreak of the Revolution, Hamilton was displaying his talents as a patriotic writer. While still a college student, he answered the writings of a persuasive New York Loyalist at about the same time that John Adams was confronting Massachusettensis in Bos-

16. Paltsits, pp. 158–59; cf. pp. 140, 161, 181.
17. Freeman, 7:403, 412, 418.

ton.[18] Soon he took up the sword and served a few months as an artillery officer until Washington made him his aide. He handled a number of delicate and tedious assignments and at last gained a command and a full share of glory at Yorktown. Hamilton was a member of Congress from New York during the final years of the war, working vigorously for stronger central government and a sound financial system. Madison, a slighter man, was more scholarly and stayed on at Princeton an extra year after taking his degree before returning to Virginia to study on his own. During the war years he helped frame the Virginia Constitution and then served a term in the state assembly. He served in Congress from 1780 to 1783 and was busy in state or national politics almost constantly thereafter. He found himself allied with Hamilton on a number of issues. The two men were temperamentally different, but both were energetic in behalf of a stronger national government.

They worked together in the Annapolis Convention of 1786; they took conspicuous leading roles at Philadelphia in 1787; and together they produced the *Federalist* papers in defense of the new Constitution. Their collaboration in this work was so close that it is still impossible to tell for certain which of them wrote certain papers.[19] When the new government under the Constitution was established, both men again found positions of leadership, Hamilton as secretary of the treasury and Madison as a leader in the House of Representatives. Thus when Washington turned to Madison and Hamilton, he was turning to the young men who knew most about the American Constitution, who in fact had participated in its establishment as deeply as he had. What is more, he must have known that, as well as being alert politicians and informed constitutionalists, both had had experience in writing appeals to the public.

Washington might well have recalled their work on the *Federalist*. When its first papers were being published, both authors had sent samples to him

18. See *A Full Vindication of the Measures of the Congress* (1774) and *The Farmer Refuted* (1775), in *The Papers of Alexander Hamilton*, ed. Harold C. Syrett and Jacob E. Cooke, 24 vols. (New York: Columbia University Press, 1961–79), 1:45–169; hereafter cited as *PAH*.

19. The authorship of the *Federalist* papers is a classic puzzle which has furrowed the brows of historians, literary experts, and even professional statisticians. I review their work briefly in *The Authority of Publius: A Reading of the Federalist Papers* (Ithaca, N.Y.: Cornell University Press, 1984), pp. 23–32.

and confidentially revealed their involvement.[20] In the end, the series ran to eighty-five papers, which were reprinted in two small volumes, and copies were sent to Mount Vernon. Of course, Washington may not have read these volumes carefully. He may have looked at only a few pages, enough to write a decent letter of appreciation.[21] But a few pages would have been enough to leave a lasting impression.

At least three aspects of the *Federalist* matched Washington's own plans for his address. First, he wanted to reach the people through the newspapers in a dignified manner. The *Federalist* had first appeared as a newspaper series interpreting constitutional issues. Second, Washington wanted to emphasize once more the importance of loyalty to the union. The *Federalist,* a thoroughgoing defense of strong national government, had opened with fourteen papers addressed to "the utility of the Union to your political prosperity." Third, Washington wanted to lessen factional disputes and elicit indulgence for his own frailties and any lingering flaws in the new constitutional government. From its first page to its last, the *Federalist* laid stress on "candor," a word used in the eighteenth century to mean goodwill or restraint from finding fault.[22]

Did Washington deliberately weigh these similarities? That seems doubtful. More likely he thought of Madison and later of Hamilton as the most helpful persons he could turn to. The *Federalist,* however, remains a monument to what the two had accomplished and to their vision, shared with Washington, of a constitutional union.

Their collaboration is all the more striking because they fell into political enmity almost as soon as the Constitution was ratified. This enmity derived in part from the particular positions they filled in the new government, but eventually their conflict involved their constitutional interpretations. The quarrel became public in further newspaper columns—with results that directly affected the Farewell Address.

The Constitution supplied a blueprint for strong national government. But it required energetic, decisive leaders to set that government in

20. Hamilton to Washington, October 30, 1787, *PAH*, 4:306; Madison to Washington, November 18, 1787, in *The Papers of James Madison*, ed. William T. Hutchinson, William M.E. Rachal, and Robert A. Rutland (Chicago: University of Chicago Press, 1962), 10:254.

21. Washington to Hamilton, August 28, 1788, in *Writings*, ed. Fitzpatrick, 30:66.

22. I have explored this aspect of the *Federalist* in *The Authority of Publius*, esp. Chap. 2.

motion and establish a harmonious working relationship among several powers. In retrospect it seems inevitable that Washington, Adams, Hamilton, Jefferson, and Madison should have had outstanding roles in the first administration. But at the time it was not clear exactly what those roles should be or what they should make of them. Washington spent some nervous first days wondering by what title the president should be called; and he and the others spent months redefining themselves in relation to one another. John Adams was vice president. From the sound of it, his office was the step just below the pinnacle of power, but its main function turned out to be presiding over the Senate. Adams in fact cast a deciding vote twenty times (a record) and exercised broad discretionary powers over crucial matters. But the daily routine was tedious: "My country has in its wisdom contrived for me the most insignificant office that ever the invention of man contrived or his imagination conceived."[23] Jefferson's place as secretary of state might also seem glamorous. His was the first executive department organized by Congress, and it was charged with the management of foreign relations. But Jefferson found that Washington exerted direct control over foreign affairs, and he watched with alarm as Hamilton expanded the Treasury and pressed his views into every area of government.

The conflict between Hamilton and Jefferson was exacerbated by external forces. One was the involvement of both men in the running newspaper war noted earlier. Another was the strain of reactions to the French Revolution. Washington's terms coincided with the upheavals in Paris and the beginnings of overt warfare between England and France. To some, the French Revolution reflected the best principles of the American struggle for liberty. To others it was a threat of anarchy against stable political institutions. The tension in Europe could not help affecting American politics, especially when both France and England laid separate claims to American sympathy and support. At moments it brought out the worst suspicions of the rivals in office. To Jefferson, Hamilton came to look like a "monarchist," a would-be prime minister to a figurehead president, engineering financial plans to enrich a large bloc in Congress and so win support for even grander schemes. To Hamilton, Jefferson

23. John Adams to Abigail Adams, December 19, 1793, in *The Works of John Adams*, ed. Charles Francis Adams, 10 vols. (Boston, 1850–56), 1:460.

seemed a head-in-the-clouds philosophe newly returned from Paris, indulging absurd and hypocritical notions of human equality when what America needed most was a strong, centralized government. But this is to express the conflict mildly. On these themes vats of poisonous ink were consumed in the press.

Washington harnessed these competing energies for a long time by the force of his own will, dignity, and talent for conciliation. But as it went on, the quarrel between Hamilton and Jefferson accelerated into much more than a personal or temporary clash. It became a persistent argument about what was most essential in the American Constitution. Was it a plan for centralized authority, a firm platform for expansive and energetic national government? Or was it a guarded, restrictive grant of powers, guaranteeing individual freedoms and local autonomy through its list of specific federal functions? These, of course, are the extremes of a range of views; looking back on the debates in the ratifying conventions one could find a dozen plausible versions of what it was the people of America had accepted. But from either of these extremes its opposite looked mortally dangerous—looked, in fact, like a conspiracy of treason.

In the end Washington had to choose; for personal and prudential reasons he sided with Hamilton. To the end of his correspondence with Jefferson he protested that fears of "monarchy" in America were both wild and insulting. "There might be *desires*," he said, but he "did not believe there were *designs* to change the form of government." And when party acrimony ran so high, it blackened and undermined Washington's own public character—"in such exaggerated and indecent terms as could scarcely be applied to a Nero; a notorious defaulter; or even to a common pickpocket."[24]

These strains rapidly led to a breach between Hamilton and Madison. The secretary of the treasury came into office with well-laid plans for national finance. Madison, after an abortive attempt to gain a Senate seat, entered the House. There he was a master at legislative maneuvering, but he had to face reelection by local taxpayers every two years. At first it seemed that the old alliance with Hamilton might offer new advantages. The Treasury would present its considered reports, and Madison would help see that Congress endorsed them. But the Constitution specifically

24. Jefferson's *Anas* for July 10, 1792 in his *Writings*, 1:199; Washington to Jefferson, July 6, 1796, in *Writings of George Washington*, 35:120.

provides that "all bills for raising revenue shall originate in the House of Representatives." Madison's personal friendship with Jefferson, his fellow Virginian, was much deeper. And of course he had a mind—and an ego—of his own.

Hamilton lost an ally, as he saw it, to the seductive wiles of Jefferson's ambitions and French ideology. In May 1792 he wrote a long detailed letter on this subject to a mutual friend.[25] Hamilton complained that he would not have become secretary of the treasury without assurance of Madison's firm support. But through rumors, innuendos, odd political maneuvers, involvement in Freneau's journalism, and at last outright attacks, Madison had shown himself to be in opposition to Hamilton and to his own earlier principles. Hamilton had now "declared openly" to Madison "my opinion of the views by which he was actuated towards me, & my determination to consider & treat him as a political enemy." Hamilton went on to protest that there was not a shadow of truth in allegations that there was a "monarchical" party plotting the overthrow of the government. The more lethal truth was unequivocal: "that Mr. Madison cooperating with Mr. Jefferson is at the head of a faction decidedly hostile to me and my administration, and actuated by views in my judgment subversive of the principles of good government and dangerous to the union, peace and happiness of the Country" (*PAH,* 11:429).

From being collaborators on the *Federalist* Hamilton and Madison had now become avowed political enemies, confronting each other publicly in new essay series on the Constitution a few months later.

The occasion was Washington's Neutrality Proclamation of 1793. Early in his second term Washington issued a brief four-paragraph statement prohibiting American citizens from aiding any of the belligerents in the current European wars and declaring a national policy of "friendly and impartial" conduct toward all the powers.[26] This statement met with murmurs of dissent, questioning the president's power to make such a proclamation as well as its wisdom and propriety. Hamilton planned a thorough defense of the president's action in eight "Pacificus" papers. These were published in the *Gazette of the United States* from June 29 to July 27. Jefferson saw the danger of this move and immediately urged Madison to

25. To Edward Carrington, May 26, 1792, in *PAH,* 11:426–45.
26. *Writings,* 32:430–31.

reply: "Nobody answers him, & his doctrines will therefore be taken for confessed. For God's sake, my dear Sir, take up your pen, select the most striking heresies and cut him to pieces in the face of the public. There is nobody else who can & will enter the lists against him."[27] The result was a series of five "Helvidius" papers in the same newspaper from August 24 to September 18.

Pacificus lists four major objections to the proclamation: it lacked constitutional authority; it violated American treaties with France; it ran contrary to gratitude to France for support during the American Revolution; and it was ill timed and unnecessary. In answer to the latter objections, Hamilton presented some hardheaded reasoning. He saw treaties with France as agreements of mutual benefit, which could not properly be invoked when France became a European aggressor and when compliance would risk America's own self-preservation. But it was the first issue that most concerned Madison when he replied—that of the constitutional grounds for the president's authority. On this point Hamilton developed a strained construction of presidential powers under the Constitution, and Madison replied strongly.

In brief, Hamilton examined the opening words of Article II of the Constitution: "The executive power shall be vested in a President of the United States of America." In these words he saw a much fuller grant of powers than the Constitution allowed to the legislature, indeed a full authorization to do everything necessary to carry out the laws and government of the nation. "The general doctrine of our constitution then is, that the executive power of the nation is vested in the president; subject only to the exceptions and qualifications, which are expressed in the instrument."[28] In the case at hand, Hamilton found no specific limitations. He noted that

27. Jefferson to Madison, July 7, 1793, in Jefferson, *Writings*, 6:338. Madison had his own reasons, too, for protesting the proclamation. He was on the verge of accepting the honor of citizenship that had been voted him in the new French Republic. See Irving Brant, *James Madison, Father of the Constitution* (Indianapolis: Bobbs, Merrill, 1950), pp. 373–74.

28. For convenience, I quote both *Pacificus* and *Helvidius* from the Gideon edition of 1845: *The Letters of Pacificus and Helvidius* (1845; reprint. Delmar, N.Y.: Scholar's Facsimiles and Reprints, 1976), p. 10; hereafter cited as *P&H*. The best explanation for these two pseudonyms is supplied by Douglass Adair: "Madison in answering Pacificus naturally did not sign himself Bellicose, but shifting the issue to Hamilton's claim for executive prerogative in foreign affairs, warned against executive tyranny in signing his essays Helvidius. As every reader of Tacitus recognized immediately, this was a reference to Helvidius Priscus, the Roman Stoic and patriot whose opposition to imperial aggrandizement first gained him banishment under Nero and, eventually, death under Vespasian" (Douglass Adair, *Fame and the Founding Fathers*, ed. Trevor Colbourn [New York: Norton 1974], p. 273n).

the Congress is empowered "to declare war, and grant letters of marque and reprisal," but he saw a thin but crucial distinction here.

> If on the one hand, the legislature have a right to declare war, it is, on the other, the duty of the executive to preserve peace, till the declaration is made; and in fulfilling this duty, it must necessarily possess a right of judging what is the nature of the obligations which the treaties of the country impose on the government: and when it has concluded that there is nothing in them inconsistent with neutrality, it becomes both its province and its duty to enforce the laws incident to that state of the nation. The executive is charged with the execution of all laws, the law of nations, as well as the municipal law, by which the former are recognised and adopted. It is consequently bound, by executing faithfully the laws of neutrality, when the country is in a neutral position, to avoid giving cause of war to foreign powers. (*P&H*, pp. 11–12)

In other words, a large area of judgment was not only left open to the president in the conduct of foreign affairs but was imposed upon him. He must do such things as declare and enforce a policy of neutrality until Congress directed otherwise. To reinforce this argument Hamilton elaborated on the president's specific duty to receive ambassadors and other public ministers. And he ended by claiming that plenary powers are implied in the president's duty to "take care that the laws be faithfully executed." But whatever its source, in Hamilton's view, the power of the executive was clearly superior to all other constitutional powers in international matters.

> It deserves to be remarked, that as the participation of the senate in the making of treaties, and the power of the legislature to declare war, are exceptions out of the general "executive power" vested in the president; they are to be construed strictly, and ought to be extended no further than is essential to their execution. (*P&H*, p.14)

Madison was not only cogent in attacking this argument; he was vehement. *Helvidius* was a direct reply to *Pacificus* and was designed to tear away its disguise and reveal its corruption. "I propose . . . to show, from the publication itself, that under colour of vindicating an important public act, of a chief magistrate who enjoys the confidence and love of his country, principles are advanced which strike at the vitals of its constitution, as well as at its honour and true interest" (*P&H*, p. 53).

As Madison read the Constitution, it is clear and specific in limiting the powers of the executive and granting important powers over treaties and international matters to Congress. Since treaties are actually laws, they belong within the legislative domain. Since the powers of making war and peace are vested in Congress, so too are the powers of determining and declaring neutrality. Instead of seeing an implied grant of plenary executive powers, Madison could see only specified presidential powers in the Constitution, and none of these supported the authority of a proclamation of neutrality. Going through *Pacificus* line by line, Madison found strained interpretations, lapses of logic, and dangerous implications hidden in plausible phrases. He concluded that *Pacificus* was a crafty attempt to exploit Washington's well-meant action, to turn it into a precedent for expanding presidential powers beyond any constitutional limit whatever. He warned that this was no idle danger: "we are to regard it as mortally certain, that as [these] doctrines make their way into the creed of the government, and the acquiescence of the public, every power that can be deduced from them, will be deduced, and exercised sooner or later by those who may have an interest in doing so" (No. 4, *P&H*, p. 86).

Moving beyond answering Pacificus, moreover, Madison attacked Hamilton more directly. By the end of the first Helvidius paper he was quoting from *Federalist* number 75, in which Hamilton had stressed that treaty making was a legislative power. And in his third and fourth papers Madison cited the *Federalist* again—on the merely ceremonial nature of the president's power to receive ambassadors, and on the dangers of giving the president sole power over treaties. In default of any solid constitutional ground for sweeping executive power, Madison could think of only one source from which Pacificus might have derived the idea: "The power of making treaties and the power of declaring war, are *royal prerogatives* in the *British government*, and are accordingly treated as *executive prerogatives* by *British commentators*" (*P&H*, p. 62). Madison could not help noticing further details throughout *Pacificus* that betrayed a "monarchist" cast of mind. Not least of these was the identification (in the seventh paper) of "the government" with the executive branch or with the president alone. Madison pounced on this "singularity of the style adopted by the writer, as showing either that the phraseology of a foreign government is more familiar to him than the phraseology proper to our own, or that he wishes to propagate a familiarity of the former in preference to the latter" (No. 5, *P&H*, p. 93). These points could not be lost on anyone who recognized Hamilton's hand in *Pacificus*. They sharply insisted that this foreign-born power seeker was now showing his true colors.

Madison went further. In the third *Helvidius* paper he rewrote the Neutrality Proclamation in a parody, as a way of showing how preposterous Pacificus's claims would be if they were not muffled in ambiguous phrases. And in the fourth paper, he forced the logic of Pacificus further yet. If, as Pacificus claimed, the president had virtually all the powers relating to war, except the strictly limited power of declaring it, then "would it be difficult to fabricate a power in the executive to plunge the nation into war, whenever a treaty of peace might happen to be infringed?" Helvidius here poses an acute question about how far a president can lead or control a government at the brink of war. Then he plunges forward with a glance at the current situation.

> But if any difficulty should arise, there is another mode chalked out, by which the end might clearly be brought about, even without the violation of the treaty of peace; especially if the other party should happen to change its government at the crisis. The executive could *suspend* the treaty of peace by *refusing to receive an ambassador* from the *new* government; and the state of war *emerges of course.* (*P&H*, p. 88)

At this time France had changed its government and Citizen Edmond Genêt had landed in America, stirring up enough trouble to make him a very unwelcome ambassador. What Madison implies here is that all the elements were in place for a reckless president to bring America to immediate ruin. The powers claimed by Pacificus, in this case for a proclamation of neutrality, could easily be manipulated for the opposite effect—to force a declaration of war.

Madison was on dangerous ground here, and he knew it. It was one thing to attack *Pacificus* by pointing out its inconsistencies, or to affront Hamilton by setting his *Federalist* pages next to his current arguments. But in attacking the Neutrality Proclamation, Madison risked slighting the president's judgment and violating his personal relations with Washington.

His consciousness of this danger made him squirm. His letters to Jefferson show him thinking up every excuse to avoid this task. He says he is too far from Philadelphia. He doubts he has the books he needs to do a proper job. He is reluctant to act because he does not know (and cannot know, and should not know) the cabinet secrets that lay behind the proclamation. Besides, Hamilton is not a man to take attacks lying down; he will be sure to engineer a keen reply. Besides, there will be delays in recopying these papers in a disguised hand, and meanwhile events are changing the meaning of what Pacificus has said. And besides, it is summer and the Virginia sun is intolerably hot. "I have forced myself into the task of a reply," he says. "I can truly say I find it the most grating one I ever experienced."[29]

Nonetheless Madison went on writing. Just a year earlier the bright sunlight had shone over his work on Washington's farewell and his own letters urging the president to remain in office. Now here he was working hand in glove with Jefferson, urging *him* to remain in office and slipping drafts to him for his perusal and correction before they were published as attacks on the president's powers. Madison might try to cover his arguments with a nice distinction: Washington's proclamation did not even mention the word "neutrality"; Pacificus was therefore building an enormous case for power out of an action that was plainly justified on other "legal and rational" grounds (*P&H*, p. 95). But this was too fine a distinction for many people to notice. Madison must have known that he was shifting his position and witnessing others shift theirs. Washington had made it plain that he wanted to leave office, his cabinet was openly divided, and the future now lay with someone else. If the choice were to be between Hamilton and Jefferson, Madison was bound to act immediately to cut the one and ally himself with the other—especially if Hamilton had the cunning to affect such proclamations and build them into elaborate doctrines of executive power!

From one aspect the debate between Pacificus and Helvidius was but an

---

29. Madison to Jefferson, July 30, 1793, in *The Writings of James Madison*, ed. Gaillard Hunt, 9 vols. (New York, 1900–10), 6:138–39n.

acute form of a larger tension. It gave expression to conflicts that were raging in other forms—in warfare between France and England; in American uncertainties about peace and the cause of liberty; in secret and overt clashes within Washington's cabinet; in conflicts between the executive branch and a newly elected Congress; in the ongoing vituperation of competing party journalists. In all these conflicts of 1793, two little newspaper series may look like a very mild skirmish.

Yet they left an indelible impression on Hamilton's memory and on Madison's and Washington's. Many years later, when Hamilton was asked to help prepare a new edition of the *Federalist*, he made a point of having *Pacificus* included as an appendix. "He remarked to me at the time," the publisher recalled, "that 'some of his friends had pronounced them to be his best performance.' "[30] Madison helped prepare the Gideon edition of 1818, which in its turn included *Helvidius*. This edition noted that all three series show Hamilton and Madison laboring in unison "to inculcate the advantages to be derived from the Constitution" and define where they later differed about "the practical construction of that instrument."[31] Meanwhile, Washington had felt the changed mood around him. His address to Congress in December 1793 narrowly defined the meaning of his proclamation—within the confines Helvidius had pronounced proper. But the president never again turned to Madison for confidential advice.[32]

When Washington again looked over his farewell, he saw Madison's draft as the work of a *former* supporter. By then Washington also saw his second term as an achievement in foreign policy. What he added to the address at this point included carefully chosen words about alliances, neutrality, and the particular dangers of political parties that favored the claims of any foreign power. In the end he addressed this point specifically: "My politicks have been unconcealed;—plain and direct.—They will be found (so far as they relate to the Belligerent Powers) in the Proclamation of 22d of April 1793; which, having met your approbation, and the confirmation of Congress, I have uniformly & steadily adhered

30. George F. Hopkins to John C. Hamilton, February 4, 1847, in *The Federalist*, ed. John C. Hamilton (Philadelphia, 1864), 1:xci–xcii.
31. *The Federalist* (Washington, D.C., 1818), p. 4.
32. Brant, pp. 386–87.

to—uninfluenced by, and regardless of, the complaints & attempts of any of those powers or their partisans to change them."[33]

Hamilton was therefore complying with Washington's orders when he expanded the address to place new and concluding emphasis on American foreign relations. In writing his draft, however, Hamilton added some noteworthy touches, including one or two passages that seem to echo the *Federalist*. In discussing the harmful effects of parties or factions, he copied the central argument of *Federalist* number 10 (a passage that Washington did not include in his final version).[34] And close to it he developed the idea that "time and habit are . . . necessary to fix the true character of governments."[35] This was a major theme in the final *Federalist* paper, too. There, an essay of David Hume's was quoted to good effect: "The judgments of many must unite in the work: EXPERIENCE must guide their labour: TIME must bring it to perfection: And the FEELING of inconveniences must correct the mistakes which they *inevitably* fall into, in their first trials and experiments." The *Federalist* then continued with lines that foreshadow some leading motifs of the Farewell Address: "These judicious reflections contain a lesson of moderation to all the sincere lovers of the union, and ought to put them upon their guard against hazarding anarchy, civil war, a perpetual alienation of the states from each other, and perhaps the military despotism of a victorious demagogue, in the pursuit of what they are not likely to obtain, but from TIME and EXPERIENCE."[36]

What then can be traced from Hamilton and Madison in the *Federalist*, to Madison and Washington in the 1792 valedictory, to Hamilton against Madison in *Pacificus* and *Helvidius*, to Hamilton and Washington in the final draft of the Farewell Address? The answer is not simple. It is complicated by personal quirks, strained friendships, changing political roles, and—in the end—the passage of time and experience in three very

33. Paltsits, p. 171. The "approbation and confirmation" of Congress refers to a neutrality statute that passed at Washington's suggestion after the controversy over his proclamation. How far the president can or should lead in matters verging on war, or should initiate any actions in the hope of congressional ratification, is still a matter of controversy. Washington's moves over neutrality are still leading precedents. See Edward S. Corwin, *The Constitution and What It Means Today*, 14th ed., rev. Harold W. Chase and Craig R. Ducat (Princeton: Princeton University Press, 1978), pp. 148, 198.

34. Paltsits, p. 189; compare revisions on pp. 203, 149.

35. Paltsits, p. 176; compare pp. 188, 148.

36. *The Federalist*, ed. Jacob E. Cooke (Middletown, Conn.: Wesleyan University Press, 1961), p. 594. Hamilton certainly understood that Hume's essays supported number 10 as well as number 85.

different human lives. Nevertheless, through the tensions and distrusts that bound these men together and drove them apart, one can perceive some common ground. Strong union; inviolable American independence; balanced government, safe from domination by any region, faction, or demagogue—these are the ideas for which all three men made sacrifices. These are the constants. The variations—which finally broke up this three-way collaboration—derived from threats to these ideals and suspicions that one or another of these public men was failing to cherish them all.

The Farewell Address repeats and once more stresses the importance of these ideals. Looked upon as a shared statement, it expresses what all three leaders had worked for in the first years under the Constitution. Hamilton and Madison did not create President Washington, and neither did he wholly direct these younger men. It was they who led the call for a Philadelphia Convention and the subsequent campaigns for a well-considered new plan of government. It was he who could summon unanimous support through two elections and hold even these divergent talents together as long as possible.

From this review of the Farewell Address, it may seem impossibly difficult to read. The story of its stages of composition, and the background of Hamilton's and Madison's involvement in it, may clutter our view—like scaffolding around a great monument. Knowledge of the scaffolding may be useful if it conveys a sense of skilled labor and careful proportions. But Washington meant to put forward a finished statement, after all. He wanted readers to consider the address as his work, his parting letter to the people, his own seal upon his presidency. In this light, the address deserves a further assessment. It must be understood as a work sui generis, a message only President Washington could have conceived and carried off. It can be compared to other addresses of a similar type—in fact, of four similar types—but in the end its features differ from all other models or analogues.

In the first place, the address is what linguists call a performative utterance, a statement that creates a new situation. When a jury pronounces a man not guilty, he is by that pronouncement released from jeopardy for an alleged crime. When Robinson Crusoe starts calling to his captive by name, the captive's name becomes Friday and he changes into a trusted servant. When Washington issued the proclamation of 1793, he seemed to commit the American government to a strict neutrality from that day forward. So when he issued his farewell: by that act, he withdrew from consideration in the coming election. He timed his statement shrewdly with that outcome in mind. But from the time of his earliest outline of a farewell, he envisioned it as much more than a brief official declaration. He used the occasion to speak both officially and unofficially—to announce his precedent-setting retirement and at the same time to take leave of his countrymen in the tone of a departing friend. On the one hand, he makes a pronouncement akin to a command: I shall not run again for president. On the other, he invites everyone to imagine him already out of office and back at Mount Vernon.

The interplay of these two identities gives the Farewell Address a peculiar double authority. Both the president and George Washington here are merged and distinct at the same time. Only the president could announce that he would not run for another term; only the president could hope to hold the attention of all the people; only the president could claim the experience and information necessary for offering advice on the most important current policies of government. Yet the decision to run or not to run was finally personal. Washington was also aware that he was the hero of the Revolution and the unanimous first choice as president. His fame and authority had been earned apart from this final office. And here he was stepping down—saying farewell to a long career. By this deed of relinquishing power he could make a unique appeal as a disinterested public servant. Master of the American government, yet servant of the American people—from this paradoxical vantage point he could press forward with lines of policy that should outlast his term.

Washington thus turns the address into an idealized outline of the presidency. He defends his own policies and actions, including his reluctant acceptance of the office. He also implies what his successors must do. The broad and best remembered phrases have this character. Parties and factions have a pernicious effect on government; the president should hold himself above party, as this president has done. War, peace, and diplomacy should grow out of firm American independence from European influence; the president should direct such foreign policy, as this president has done. The president should be answerable to the people and not hold office permanently; he should transfer power gracefully, as this president is about to do.

There are similar appeals and pronouncements in addresses by other presidents. Jefferson came into office in 1801 with the famous declaration that he and the people should be united above party: "We are all Republicans, we are all Federalists." Other leaders have found lofty justification for exercising powers that neither the Constitution nor the laws specifically provided. But such statements are most common in inaugural speeches or in the midst of a pressing need—in other words, at times when a president needs to consolidate support before taking action. Their recurrence in a final address can only recall the larger outlines of what Washington said here. His farewell is unique because it is the first and because he closed his term with firm assertion of constitutional powers. The address interprets and thereby ratifies Washington's two administrations—the first, as the establishment of a sound domestic government; the second, as the proper course through international tensions. The address describes a large and complete framework of explicit and unquestionable accomplishments—all attributable to the president.

Washington could not find a model for such an address in America, at least none more famous than his own Legacy circular to the states at the end of the war. The Farewell Address has been compared, however, to the political testaments that European rulers composed throughout the eighteenth century. It was customary for a monarch to put together a statement of his observations and long-range policies to serve as a summation of his experience in power and as a guide to his successor. Earlier (in chapter 4) we noted Prince Frederick of Great Britain writing out such a testament for the future George III, just after the royal performance of *Cato* in 1749. Other royal testaments became famous when they eventually reached print, such as the two versions of the testament of Frederick the Great of Prussia. Felix Gilbert has argued that this tradition of royal testaments influenced Washington's farewell; he claims that "in revising Washington's draft for a valedictory, Hamilton transformed it into a Political Testament" of this sort.[37]

But in at least two ways political testaments were sharply different from

37. Felix Gilbert, *To the Farewell Address* (Princeton: Princeton University Press, 1961), p. 134.

what Washington sent to the press. They were secret documents, usually securely hidden away for reasons of state; sometimes their frank assessments of political realities could not be revealed even after their authors were long dead.[38] And if they were publishable at all, their earliest appearance was after the death of a monarch. By contrast, Washington's farewell was designed for immediate and widespread reading at a time of a peaceful transfer of power through a free election. Washington may have closed with a sense of his impending death, but he yearned to be out of office well before it occurred. If he or Hamilton entertained thoughts of European testaments, they recast them into an American departure from that form.

There is one final analogue that does recall a European monarch, but not of the eighteenth century nor perhaps of any time. As we noted in reviewing Washington's changing ideas of the address, he both chose to retire and felt impelled to it by duty and the weight of age. Few kings have ever abdicated or left high power, unless at the point of defeat or unspeakable outrage. As Sophocles and Shakespeare understood, such rites of passage are the stuff of high tragedy. There is a touch of the sublime in yielding up power with grace.

The closest approach to it may be the opening scene in *King Lear*, where the old king has staged a great ceremony for the conclusion of his reign. He will preside to the last over what is inevitable, and "publish" his bequests while still alive.

> Know that we have divided
> In three our kingdom; and 'tis our fast intent
> To shake all cares and business from our age,
> Conferring them on younger strengths, while we
> Unburdened crawl toward death.
>
> (1.1.38–42)

In these few lines the character begins his descent from the majesty of command to the debility of his "crawl toward death." He too would escape high office before becoming incompetent and would manage its transfer wisely—"that future strife / May be prevented now" (1.1.45–46). But

---

38. Gilbert, pp. 100, 163–64. Frederick the Great's testaments were not printed in full until the twentieth century; they are conveniently summarized in English in G. P. Gooch, *Frederick the Great: The Ruler, the Writer, the Man* (London and New York: Longmans, Green, 1947), Chap. 13.

Lear learns all too well what Washington learned, too, in his relations with Hamilton and Madison. Letting go of well-managed power is a long step toward grief. Lear relinquishes a divided kingdom and lives on to see his world shattered by warfare; Washington was to witness a surge of party hatreds in the years he had left.

Still, history is rarely as neat or as devastating as tragedy. General Washington was not exactly Cato, not was President Washington an American Lear. He succeeded in reclaiming his comforts along the Potomac—despite an awkward return to military duty in 1798. The farewell was his last great public message, as he had meant it to be. When he died in 1799 he left a strong union in the hands of younger men, including Adams, Jefferson, and Madison.

Jefferson's Trinity

Thomas Jefferson has become the legendary intellectual among American statesmen: the model of the philosopher-president, the man who could outlive power and retire gracefully to a larger life among his books, thoughts, and architectural innovations. This legend was reinforced not long ago in President John F. Kennedy's famous line delivered at a dinner for Nobel Prize winners: "This is the most extraordinary collection of talent, of human knowledge, that has ever been gathered together at the White House, with the possible exception of when Thomas Jefferson dined alone."[1] Long before the Kennedy dinner, Jefferson himself had sealed the same impression. He left clear instructions for the epitaph that still appears over his grave:

Here was buried Thomas Jefferson
Author of the Declaration of American Independence
Of the Statute of Virginia for religious freedom
And Father of the University of Virginia

"Not a word more," he stipulated: not a word about being president, vice president, secretary of state, minister to France, or governor of Virginia.[2]

---

1. "Remarks at a Dinner Honoring Nobel Prize Winners of the Western Hemisphere," April 29, 1962, in *Public Papers of the Presidents of the United States: John F. Kennedy, 1962* (Washington, D.C.,: U.S. Government Printing Office, 1963), p. 347.

2. Jefferson's 1826 instructions for his monument have often been reprinted and reproduced, e.g., as the frontispiece to *The Life and Selected Writings of Thomas Jefferson*, ed. Adrienne Koch and William

These four lines associate his name only with acts of the mind: the declaration, a guarantee of freedom of thought, the founding of a university.

But on close inspection, Jefferson's intellect was not that extraordinary. President Kennedy went on to describe a man of all talents: "Someone once said that Thomas Jefferson was a gentleman of 32 who could calculate an eclipse, survey an estate, tie an artery, plan an edifice, try a cause, break a horse, and dance the minuet." But with only a few substitutions the same description might fit young Washington or Adams or Hamilton; it might fit Franklin with even less alteration. The achievements engraved on his tombstone were not his alone. The declaration was assigned to Jefferson by a committee of Congress and was amended considerably before it passed. The Virginia statute was the work of many hands. And the University of Virginia was a cooperative enterprise, founded and established by the union of many talents, not "fathered" by one man alone. Besides, Franklin could lay a rival claim to fathering the University of Pennsylvania; and Washington was so keen to establish a national university that he made a point of mentioning it in the Farewell Address.

Jefferson left no science behind him, like Franklin's science of electricity; he was hardly what we would call a philosopher or poet; yet neither was he a mere amateur or collector. He applied his mind to the scholarship of many fields, relating and adapting them to emerging conditions in America. He was seldom original, but always observant and often ingenious at bringing people and ideas together in ways that prospered. At times he seems to have been a remote, isolated thinker, but he was also an active sociable man. Monticello remains his proper monument. The entrance hall to the west, adorned with trophies and specimens of the Lewis and Clark expedition, is only thinly divided from the parlor to the east, full of treasures acquired in Paris. And both rooms open to a dining room that was conveniently fitted up for many guests. Even in his secluded cabinet and library, Jefferson was hardly alone. He would read the latest books from the learned world, write to correspondents at great distances, and lay out plans for a busy farm and a university.

One day in 1811 he sat down to record an anecdote that described his

Peden, (New York: Modern Library 1944). I copy the inscription as it now appears on the grave, according to Frederick D. Nichols and James A. Bear, Jr., *Monticello: A Guidebook* (Monticello, Va.,: Thomas Jefferson Memorial Foundation, 1982), p. 68.

own ideal of mental achievement. He named Francis Bacon, Isaac Newton, and John Locke as his trinity of "the three greatest men the world had ever produced." And he narrated how he had invoked these three heroes in a dramatic confrontation with Alexander Hamilton, a clash in which Jefferson triumphed. This little story reveals a lot about Jefferson, and it deserves to be examined in several lights.

To begin, I will quote his account at length. In its immediate context, it is the conclusion of a two-part story about Jefferson, John Adams, and Hamilton at a cabinet meeting in 1791, when Jefferson was secretary of state.

> I received a letter from President Washington, then at Mount Vernon, desiring me to call together the Heads of departments, and to invite Mr. Adams to join us (which, by-the-bye, was the only instance of that being done) in order to determine on some measure which required despatch; and he desired me to act on it, as decided, without again recurring to him. I invited them to dine with me, and after dinner, sitting at our wine, having settled our question, other conversation came on, in which a collision of opinion arose between Mr. Adams and Colonel Hamilton, on the merits of the British constitution, Mr. Adams giving it as his opinion, that, if some of its defects and abuses were corrected, it would be the most perfect constitution of government ever devised by man. Hamilton, on the contrary, asserted, that with its existing vices, it was the most perfect model of government that could be formed; and that the correction of its vices would render it an impracticable government. And this you may be assured was the real line of difference between the political principles of these two gentlemen.

So far, the conflict lies between Hamilton and Adams, with Adams being rebuffed. But now Jefferson moves in to reverse the situation.

> Another incident took place on the same occasion, which will further delineate Mr. Hamilton's political principles. The room being hung around with a collection of the portraits of remarkable men, among them were those of Bacon, Newton and Locke. Hamilton asked me who they were. I told him they were my trinity of the three greatest

men the world had ever produced, naming them. He paused for some time: "the greatest man," said he, "that ever lived, was Julius Caesar."

The next line gives the moral of the tale: "Mr. Adams was honest as a politician, as well as a man; Hamilton honest as a man, but, as a politician, believing in the necessity of either force or corruption to govern men."[3] But the power of the story lies in the rhythmic pauses and suspense of Hamilton's reply. Hamilton is blackened here in several ways. In the first encounter he roundly approves the "vices" of the British government. In the second, he moves from admitting his ignorance of three famous men to revealing his own ideal of fame. When Jefferson wrote this story in 1811, it also carried some heavy overtones. Hamilton had died by violence in 1804, in his duel with Aaron Burr. And another Caesar-like villain had cast his shadow across Europe. Napoleon in fact had risen like Hamilton, emerging from obscurity to high power as a heroic young officer in a revolution. Jefferson among others had noted the similarity.[4]

But in its larger context this anecdote deals with Hamilton only in passing. The story occurs in a long letter to Benjamin Rush, the Philadelphia doctor and patriot. Jefferson is here answering Rush's efforts to reconcile the two former presidents, Jefferson and Adams, by providing a detailed account of their past relations. Jefferson writes:

> I receive with sensibility your observations on the discontinuance of friendly correspondence between Mr. Adams and myself, and the concern you take in its restoration. This discontinuance has not proceeded from me, nor from the want of sincere desire and of effort on my part, to renew our intercourse. You know the perfect coincidence of principle and of action, in the early part of the Revolution, which produced a high degree of mutual respect and esteem between Mr.

3. Jefferson to Dr. Benjamin Rush, January 16, 1811, in *The Writings of Thomas Jefferson*, ed. Paul Leicester Ford, 10 vols. (New York, 1892–99), 9:295–96; hereafter cited as *WTJ*. This printed version accurately transcribes Jefferson's words but changes some spellings and abbreviations and capitalizes the first words of sentences, as Jefferson habitually did not. The incidents described here took place on Monday, April 11, 1791, according to John A. Schutz and Douglass Adair, eds., *The Spur of Fame: Dialogues of John Adams and Benjamin Rush, 1805–1813* (San Marino, Calif.: Huntington Library, 1966), p. 1. Washington's plan of leaving matters to his cabinet in his absence is discussed in Douglas Southall Freeman, *George Washington* (New York: Scribners, 1954), 6:304–06.

4. Dumas Malone, *Jefferson and His Time*, 6 vols. (Boston: Little Brown, 1948–81), 3:440–41. Malone also notes that Hamilton compared Jefferson to Caesar in 1792 (2:287n).

Adams and myself. Certainly no man was ever truer than he was, in that day, to those principles of rational republicanism which, after the necessity of throwing off our monarchy, dictated all our efforts in the establishment of a new government. And although he swerved, afterwards, towards the principles of the English constitution, our friendship did not abate on that account. (*WTJ*, 9:295)

The anecdote is thus framed by Jefferson's effort to recall Adams and emphasize his best points. He begins at a point of "perfect coincidence" between the two men, both "of principles and of action." The principles that united them were those of "rational republicanism," and they lasted from the first stages of the Revolution through the rejection of monarchy and into the newly established American government. But then Adams "swerved" toward different principles, "towards the principles of the English constitution," apparently leaving Jefferson alone as a true rational republican. The anecdotes serve to measure just how far this divergence went. Hamilton serves as a foil. The first collision with him shows that Adams was far from being a thoroughgoing admirer of British monarchy; he saw defects and abuses, which Hamilton approved. The second collision dramatizes Jefferson's firm orthodoxy. He stood surrounded by the heroes of enlightened rationality. Hamilton did not even recognize them; his model was Julius Caesar.

The letter goes on to explain that Adams and Jefferson split on precisely these matters of principle.

You remember the machinery which the federalists played off, about that time, to beat down the friends to the real principles of our constitution, to silence by terror every expression in their favor, to bring us into war with France and alliance with England, and finally to homologize our constitution with that of England. Mr. Adams, you know, was overwhelmed with feverish addresses, dictated by the fear, and often by the pen, of the *bloody buoy*, and was seduced by them into some open indications of his new principles of government.[5]

5. *WTJ*, 9:296. I have not been able to ascertain the meaning of the phrase *bloody buoy*; my reasoned guess is that it refers here to a High Federalist group or person (who could wield a pen), e.g., Timothy Pickering or Hamilton or a newspaper editor. Jefferson's *Anas* also contains this phrase in describing the scare tactics of Federalist propaganda: "The horrors of the French Revolution, then

This clash of principles led to Adams's defeat in the election of 1800. Jefferson recalled telling Adams at the time that he took no personal satisfaction from having defeated his old friend.

> "Mr. Adams," said I, "this is no personal contest between you and me. Two systems of principles on the subject of government divide our fellow citizens into two parties. With one of these you concur, and I with the other. As we have been longer on the public stage than most of those now living, our names happen to be more generally known. One of these parties, therefore, has put your name at its head, the other mine. Were we both to die to-day, to-morrow two other names would be in the place of ours, without any change in the motion of the machinery. Its motion is from principle, not from you or myself." (*WTJ*, 9:296–97)

Where Adams and Jefferson stood in relation to Hamilton was therefore an index of where they stood on matters of principle. And that in turn was what determined their public careers and their personal relations. Adams was "overwhelmed" while Jefferson stood firm. Adams became irritated (and so did Mrs. Adams) in defeat; Jefferson remained clear-sighted, recognizing that despite passing political differences there were still solid grounds for personal cordiality and esteem.

This account of Adams and Jefferson is obviously colored by egotism as well as generosity. As he names Adams's strengths, Jefferson does not stint at highlighting his own, including his greater readiness to separate feelings from politics. All his emphases on principle also point to an odd strain of character. At one moment he seems to efface himself and become a mere figurehead of party, an easily replaced cog "of the machinery." Yet he is also emphatically much more than that. His principles are the winning principles; they have been endorsed by the people; they are the principles of Locke, not Caesar; they are also the earliest principles of the Revolution, from which Jefferson has never "swerved." Such merging of

---

raging, aided them mainly, and using that as a raw head and bloody bones they were enabled by their stratagems of X. Y. Z., . . . their tales of tub-plots, Ocean massacres, bloody buoys, . . . to spread alarm into all but the firmest breasts" (*WTJ*, 1:167). In any case it is a striking phrase for Jefferson to emphasize in a letter to Rush, whose medical theories in favor of phlebotomy had made him notorious as a bloody doctor. Rush had sued William Cobbett for libel in 1797 as part of a long and bitter effort to restore his reputation. See Lyman Butterfield, ed., *Letters of Benjamin Rush*, 2 vols. (Princeton: Princeton University Press, 1951), 2:1213–18.

self and high principle makes this version of history suspicious. The full publication of Hamilton's writings has revealed that he seldom mentioned Caesar, and never favorably.[6] And there is room to doubt that Jefferson spoke quite so finely to Adams about the meaning of defeat.

Nonetheless, this letter and its anecdote still contain nuggets worth further refining. By presenting Rush with such a full account of his feelings, Jefferson took a long step toward reviving his friendship with Adams. And by going out of his way to record this confrontation with Hamilton, he drew a tidy vignette of himself. Each of these results deserves more explication.

In writing to Rush, Jefferson was picking up the threads that connected Monticello to the Adams household in Massachusetts. Rush had long been writing to both ex-presidents and urging them to write to each other. At the same time, he had kept their confidences and continued to receive frank and friendly letters from both sides. He had elicited long and unsparing accounts from Adams of incidents and characters from his past. In return, Rush confided some of his own dreams. Soon after Jefferson retired from the presidency in 1809, he dreamed that renewed correspondence between Adams and Jefferson would go on for years, and contain the riches of both men's thoughts. "These gentlemen," his dream-narrative concluded, "sunk into the grave nearly at the same time, full of years and rich in the gratitude and praises of their country (for they outlived the heterogeneous parties that were opposed to them), and to their numerous merits and honors posterity has added that they were rival friends."[7]

Rush's dream came true largely because of his constant efforts. He was in a position to filter out the harsh remarks and pass along the abiding respect each man expressed toward the other. He also prodded each correspondent to review his long association with the other, to turn over in his mind the substantial history of their shared hopes, feelings, and achievements. At the same time, other events were working to bring them together. Shortly after Jefferson wrote to Rush in 1811, two of his neighbors

6. Thomas Govan, "Alexander Hamilton and Julius Caesar: A Note on the Use of Historical Evidence," *William and Mary Quarterly*, 3 ser., 32 (1975): 475–80. Douglass Adair has also pointed out that there was a long-standing hierarchy of fame—endorsed by Bacon in his *Essays* and later by Hume—that subordinated philosophers to men like Caesar, *conditores imperiorum*, founders of states and commonwealths. Hamilton's reply could therefore have been sharp rather than ignorant or brutal. See Adair, *Fame and the Founding Fathers*, ed. Trevor Colbourne (New York: Norton, 1974), pp. 13–20.

7. Rush to Adams, October 16, 1809, in Schutz and Adair, p. 157.

visited Adams in Massachusetts and brought home a friendly report. Their conversations had included a recollection of Jefferson's visits to Adams in 1800 that exactly matched the account he had given Rush. Adams acknowledged that Jefferson had treated him courteously in defeat and had separated party differences from personal regard. "I always loved Jefferson," Adams exclaimed, "and still love him." At the end of the year Jefferson avowed, "This is enough for me."[8] Early in 1812 Adams took up his pen and soon he and Jefferson were exchanging letters steadily. Their friendship continued until 1826, when both died on the Fourth of July, the fiftieth anniversary of the Declaration of Independence.

Their renewed friendship remains a noble chapter in the American political tradition. Adams's defeat in 1800 was so bitter to him that he sped home from Washington to avoid Jefferson's inauguration. And in his long letter to Rush, Jefferson still found it hard to forgive the sabotage Adams left behind. "The last day of his political power, the last hours, and even beyond the midnight, were employed in filling all offices, and especially permanent ones, with the bitterest federalists, and providing for me the alternative, either to execute the government by my enemies, whose study it would be to thwart and defeat all my measures, or to incur the odium of such numerous removals from office, as might bear me down" (*WTJ*, 9:297–98). Not many years later, however, this enmity ran its course. Jefferson too left the presidency and found in Adams the one other man who knew that experience. Energetic correspondence became the fitting conclusion to their years of rivalry.[9]

They took up their pens for much more than a token exchange of greetings. Their letters developed into a solid correspondence—in more senses than one. They wrote long letters, catching up strands of reminiscence, shared reading, and constant mental activity. Before long they were turning to one another across the distance of many miles as reliable companions in the business of life. Thus they recalled and furthered the ways they had matched one another through all the principal seasons of

8. Jefferson to Rush, December 5, 1811, *WTJ*, 9:300n. The fullest account of this reconciliation is still L. H. Butterfield, "The Dream of Benjamin Rush: The Reconciliation of John Adams and Thomas Jefferson," *Yale Review*, n.s. 40 (1950–51): 297–319.

9. Adams told Rush that a farewell like Washington's was a gesture beyond his capacities (Schutz and Adair, p. 194); but running accounts of his life and ideals often busied him for hours with many correspondents.

their careers. Though born in far separated pockets of colonial America, they had shared similar patterns of experience through the Revolution and its consequences. Both had been early activists, making informed legal arguments for colonists' rights against Parliament and joining forces in the first Continental Congresses. Both had put their energies into the drafting of state constitutions. Both had served long diplomatic missions in Europe, thereby missing the deliberations and debates that brought forth the federal Constitution. Both had returned to become leading officers in Washington's administrations, before Jefferson followed Adams into the offices of vice president and president. They had often written, visited, and depended on each other, befriended each other's children, consoled each other's griefs. Now in old age both took their comforts in farming and books, at Monticello and at the Quincy homestead Adams came to style "Montezillo."

Adams initiated the first exchange with a deft touch of generosity. He sent a bit of New England "homespun" as he called it, which Jefferson discovered was a set of books: *Lectures in Rhetoric and Oratory* by John Quincy Adams. The younger Adams had already stood out as a lone Federalist senator in favor of some of Jefferson's policies; these recent Harvard lectures showed that a new generation could combine politics and learning. This first gift also set a bookish tone for what would follow. "I have given up newspapers," Jefferson wrote in his first letter, "in exchange for Tacitus and Thucydides, for Newton and Euclid; and I find myself much the happier." Adams exclaimed that this exchange was a movement from the depths of bathos to the contemplation of the heaven of heavens. "Oh that I had devoted to Newton and his Fellows that time, which I fear has been wasted on Plato and Aristotle, Bacon, . . . Bolingbroke, De Lolme, Harrington, Sidney, Hobbes."[10] And so their letters took up a constant theme of serious reading.

Embedded in these first lists of authors were Bacon and Newton, if not Locke. But with a subtle difference. Jefferson's trinity would never be well regarded by Adams, despite his polite exclamations. And Adams was seeking a heaven of heavens that lay beyond Jefferson's imagination.

To Jefferson, as to many eighteenth-century learned men, "Bacon,

10. Lester J. Cappon, ed., *The Adams-Jefferson Letters*, 2 vols. (Chapel Hill: University of North Carolina Press, 1959), II, 291, 294: hereafter cited as Cappon.

Newton, and Locke" was a formula for an ideal of human progress. Bacon had established a modern method of observation and inductive reasoning. Newton and Locke had used these methods to disclose the laws of the physical universe and of human nature. Jefferson and others believed that these three minds had transformed the world of learning, creating new platforms for modern philosophy, science, and politics. But anyone who studied these three authors in detail or read widely in history and science knew better. Three thinkers alone could not have done so much. But these three names in this order stood for a new attitude to learning. To the eighteenth century they were the founders of a new era, such as Darwin, Marx, Freud, and Einstein have seemed in our day. Voltaire pointed to Bacon, Newton, and Locke as the greatest men who ever lived in his *Lettres Philosophiques* (1734); d'Alembert amplified their praises in the Preliminary Discourse to the *Encyclopedia*; thereafter no self-respecting intellectual could avoid the force of their names.

Jefferson not only knew them; he went to some effort to honor them. While he was in Europe he went out of his way to seek their images. From Paris he wrote to John Trumbull in London, asking for an estimate for pictures or plaster busts of Newton, Locke, Bacon, Sydney, Hampden, and Shakespeare. A few days later he wrote that he would forego the others— "all of them except Bacon, Locke, and Newton, whose pictures I will trouble you to have copied for me." He insisted on these: "As I consider them the three greatest men that have ever lived, without any exception, and as having laid the foundation of those superstructures which have been raised in the Physical and Moral sciences, I would wish to form them into a knot on the same canvas, that they may not be confounded at all with the herd of other great men." What he had in mind was a large oval containing three oval portraits. Each figure was to be a bust "the size of the life"; the composite painting would have been four or five feet high. Jefferson made a sketch with Bacon's oval above the other two, Locke's to the left and Newton's to the right: "Bacon at top Locke next then Newton." Trumbull pointed out that such a large oval full of ovals would make an unwieldy canvas, so Jefferson relented and ordered three separate pictures.[11] But he had played with a grand idea of carrying Bacon, New-

11. Jefferson to John Trumbull, January 18 and February 15, 1789, *The Papers of Thomas Jefferson*, ed. Julian P. Boyd (Princeton: Princeton University Press, 1958), 14:467–68, 561.

ton, and Locke back to America in impressive form. If Hamilton paused before their pictures a few years later and dared to ask who they were, no wonder Jefferson replied as he did.

Jefferson also carried these heroes in his mind. He organized the books in his library according to categories laid out by Bacon. He collected and recorded observations of natural phenomena. He cherished the idea of living by the best modern principles, of taking part in the liberation of men's minds from the ignorance and superstitions of past ages. He believed in progress, and he liked to think that the American and French revolutions were stages in its unfolding.

Adams turned a much colder eye on modern progressivism. In general he read history with a deep skepticism about progress, while Jefferson too readily claimed to be part of its steady liberation of the human mind. Within the first year of their renewed dialogue this strain between them became evident.

Jefferson bluntly recalled Adams's well-known conversatism:

> One of the questions you know on which our parties took different sides, was on the improvability of the human mind, in science, in ethics, in government etc. Those who advocated reformation of institutions, pari passu, with the progress of science, maintained that no definite limits could be assigned to that progress. The enemies of reform, on the other hand, denied improvement, and advocated steady adherence to the principles, practices and institutions of our fathers, which they represented as the consummation of wisdom, and akmé of excellence, beyond which the human mind could never advance. Altho' in [an address Adams had made as president, to the young men of Philadelphia], you expressly disclaim the wish to influence the freedom of enquiry, you predict that that will produce nothing more worthy of transmission to posterity, than the principles, institutions, and systems of education received from their ancestors. (Cappon, 2:332)

In return, Adams called belief in revolutionary progress a mad espousal of "ideology" (Cappon, 2:355). He continued to doubt that millions of people could be aroused, let alone educated in one generation, to a new and more enlightened social order.

While all other Sciences have advanced, that of Government is at a stand; little better understood; little better practiced now than 3 or 4 thousand Years ago. What is the Reason? I say Parties and Factions will not suffer, or permit Improvements to be made. As soon as one Man hints at an improvement his Rival opposes it. No sooner has one Party discovered or invented an Amelioration of the Condition of Man or the order of Society, than the opposite Party, belies it, miscon- strues it, misrepresents it, ridicules it, insults it, and persecutes it. Records are destroyed. Histories are annihilated or interpolated, or prohibited sometimes by Popes, sometimes by Emperors, sometimes by Aristocratical and sometimes by democratical Assemblies and sometimes by Mobs. (Cappon, 2:351)

Adams could speak out bluntly, too:

Let me now ask you, very seriously my Friend, Where are now in 1813, the Perfection and perfectability of human Nature? Where is now, the progress of the human Mind? Where is the Amelioration of Society? Where the Augmentations of human Comforts? Where the diminutions of human Pains and miseries? . . .

When? Where? and how? is the present Chaos to be arranged into Order? (Cappon, 2:358)

Adams had long been reading the most current theorists of progress and recording his doubts and rejoinders in the margins of their books. If Jefferson's mind turned readily to secular scientific discoveries, Adams's returned to lasting verities. As time went on he revealed that he was reading much more than Jefferson was and working assiduously to recon- cile the skepticism of the Enlightenment with an abiding Christian faith— of a kind Jefferson never experienced.[12]

The tone of their correspondence therefore became intricate as months went by. Both writers knew that these personal letters might well be published years hence. They were on their mettle to be affectionate and entertaining and to strengthen the bonds they had at last renewed. But they

12. On Adams's wide reading and marginal annotations, see Zoltán Haraszti, *John Adams and the Prophets of Progress* (Cambridge, Mass.: Harvard University Press, 1952); on his studies of the gods, see Frank E. Manuel, *The Eighteenth Century Confronts the Gods* (Cambridge, Mass.: Harvard University Press, 1959), pp. 271–80.

were also conscious of being different men, with much at stake in their efforts to explain themselves to each other. Often they would contradict themselves from one letter to another, softening their words one week only to hammer at the same points a few days later. Each man also stretched to match or accommodate the other's vitality and interests.

Their distinct contours still emerge unmistakably in these pages. Jefferson's high principles, which he had stressed to Rush, ran counter to Adams's unwavering principles, which he dug out and quoted verbatim from his address to the young men of Philadelphia. "Without wishing to damp the Ardor of curiosity, or influence the freedom of inquiry, I will hazard a prediction, that after the most industrious and impartial Researches, the longest liver of you all, will find no Principles, Institutions, or Systems of Education, more fit, IN GENERAL to be transmitted to your posterity, than those you have received from your Ancestors" (Cappon, 2:339). Adams went on to insist to Jefferson that these were loose, general principles—not the products of refined modern intellect, but common moral understandings diffused throughout society. "And what were these *general Principles?* I answer, the general Principles of Christianity, in which all those Sects were United: And the *general Principles* of English and American Liberty, in which all those young Men United, and which had United all Parties in America, in Majorities sufficient to assert and maintain her Independence." They were none the less true for being so widespread:

> Now I will avow, that I then believed, and now believe, that those general Principles of Christianity, are as eternal and immutable, as the Existence and Attributes of God; and that those Principles of Liberty, are as unalterable as human Nature and our terrestrial, mundane System. I could therefore safely say, consistently with all my then and present Information, that I believed they would never make Discoveries in contradiction to these *general Principles*. In favour of these *general Principles* in Phylosophy, Religion and Government, I could fill Sheets of quotations from Frederick of Prussia, from Hume, Gibbon, Bolingbroke, Reausseau and Voltaire, as well as Neuton and Locke. (Cappon, 2:340)

Even seven years later this conflict was unabated. Jefferson wrote: "Mr. Locke, you know, and other materialists have charged with blasphemy the

Spiritualists who have denied to the Creator the power of endowing certain forms of matter with the faculty of thought. These however are speculations and subtleties in which, for my own part, I have little indulged myself. When I meet with a proposition beyond finite comprehension, I abandon it as I do a weight which human strength cannot lift: and I think ignorance, in these cases, is truly the softest pillow on which I can lay my head" (Cappon, 2:562). Adams—now eighty-eight years old—was still ready with a reply.

> I confess I know not how Spirit can think, feel or act, any more than Matter. In truth, I cannot conceive how either can move or think, so that I must repose upon your pillow of ignorance, which I find very soft and consoleing, for it absolves my conscience from all cupability in this respect. But I insist upon it that the Saint has as good a right to groan at the Philosopher for asserting that there is nothing but matter in the Universe, As the Philosopher has to laugh at the Saint for saying that there are both Matter and Spirit. (Cappon, 2:564)

Thus, though both men knew Newton and Locke and dozens of other modern thinkers—could cite them in detail or quickly track them in the well-thumbed volumes in their libraries—when they turned toward each other they clung to different worlds. Jefferson remained true to his trinity and doubtless kept them in mind as he planned and fostered a modern university. But Adams remained true to his right to laugh while puzzling over more than matter in the universe. By a long and involved development Jefferson spent his final fifteen years in the same posture he had described to Rush in 1811. He was armed with the same heroes to face a political antagonist. But in Adams, unlike Hamilton, he addressed a scholar every bit his equal—one eager and resourceful to maintain that these were *not* the greatest men the world had ever produced.

Jefferson's heroes come under even harsher light in the writings of another contemporary who devoted himself to pitched battle against them. This was the English poet and artist, William Blake. Blake is often considered a romantic poet of the late eighteenth century, akin to Wordsworth and Coleridge. But his life span (1757–1827) nicely overlaps that of Jefferson (1743–1826) or Adams (1735–1826). Adams and Jefferson sometimes indulged one another because they recognized that the conservative was somewhat older and the ideologue somewhat younger. Blake was younger still, and yet closer to Adams in his spiritual longings and in the acid wit of his outrage. He had grown up in the London of Dr. Johnson, Edmund Burke, Sir Joshua Reynolds, and Oliver Goldsmith, and come of age with the American and French revolutions. He may have known Joseph Priestly, Thomas Paine, and William Godwin personally, and he read the works of dozens of modern social critics.[13] Yet he pitted his soul against Jefferson's trio of heroes. For him Bacon, Newton, and Locke were symbols of all that was wrong in the modern world—though the American and French revolutions seemed hopeful signs of a new birth of human freedom. Jefferson's trinity has to be seen at last against the poetry Blake made of them—poetry that even took one or two touches from Jefferson's own works.

Blake hated Newton and Locke because of the way he understood reality. In part, his anger may have sprung from his practice as a professional artist and engraver. His daily work was to produce images of the world, and modern materialism reduced this work to absurdity. If Newton and Locke were right about the mind's passive acceptance of sense impressions of outer objects, then art was mere triviality. It was the tracing of inert matter, the flattery of human poses, or the skilled coloring of idle daydreams. Against this range of possibilities Blake became fierce and fought back with a sense of religious mission. He was what his time called an enthusiastic zealot. A century earlier he might have been a radical Puritan (in his later work he claims to be corporeally and spiritually joined with John Milton). As it was, he felt the realities of spiritual life being smothered under the presuppositions of modern science. The progression from Bacon to Newton to Locke was far from a liberation of the human mind; it was a dreary invasion of the living universe of God and man. Scientific skepticism led to cold materialism and then to mere psychology and the social ordering of automatons. Each step implied the stages to follow, and the end of all was the earth as a mindless planet of

13. Blake's relationship to these writers in the early 1790s was through the weekly dinners of the bookseller Joseph Johnson, who published their works and employed Blake as an engraver. See Mona Wilson, *The Life of William Blake*, ed. Geoffrey Keynes (London: Oxford University Press, 1971), pp. 44–47; and David V. Erdman, *Blake: Prophet against Empire*, 3d ed. (Princeton: Princeton University Press, 1977), pp. 154–57; the latter hereafter cited as Erdman.

rock drifting in a random cosmos. This was the dismal worldview that Blake combated, styling himself a biblical prophet or visionary and styling his opponents sometimes as "Bacon & Newton & Locke," sometimes as Antichrist.

One of his marginal notes in Reynolds's *Discourses* expresses these ideas in Blake's typically vigorous language:

> Burke's Treatise on the Sublime & Beautiful is founded on the Opinions of Newton & Locke; on this Treatise Reynolds has grounded many of his assertions in all his Discourses. I read Burke's Treatise when very Young; at the same time I read Locke on Human Understanding & Bacon's Advancement of Learning; on Every one of these Books I wrote my Opinions, & on looking them over find that my Notes on Reynolds in this Book are exactly Similar. I felt the Same Contempt & Abhorrence then that I do now. They mock Inspiration & Vision. Inspiration & Vision was then, & now is, & I hope will always Remain, my Element, my Eternal Dwelling place; how can I then hear it Contemned without returning Scorn for Scorn?[14]

Blake's poetry gave form to this visionary argument. His long final work, *Jerusalem*, represented mankind as a giant named Albion, slumbering in the torpor of sensual perception and suffering the tortures of unrelenting necessity.

> I see the Past, Present & Future existing all at once
> Before me. O Divine Spirit, sustain me on thy wings,
> That I may awake Albion from his long & cold repose;
> For Bacon & Newton, sheath'd in dismal steel, their terrors hang
> Like iron scourges over Albion: Reasonings like vast Serpents
> Infold around my limbs, bruising my minute articulations.
> I turn my eyes to the Schools & Universities of Europe
> And there behold the Loom of Locke, whose Woof rages dire,
> Wash'd by the Water-wheels of Newton: black the cloth
> In heavy wreathes folds over every Nation: cruel Works
> Of many Wheels I view, wheel without wheel, with cogs tyrannic

14. William Blake, *Complete Writings*, ed. Geoffrey Keynes (London: Oxford University Press, 1966), pp. 476–77. All quotations of Blake are from this edition.

Moving by compulsion each other, not as those in Eden, which,
Wheel within Wheel, in freedom revolve in harmony & peace.

(Plate 15)

The cogs of Newtonian reasoning, like the cogs of an industrial loom, spin
out a pall over learning. But Blake, a prophet like Ezekiel of old, invokes
the divine spirit in order to awaken men from such "long & cold repose."

These quotations barely suffice as touchstones of Blake's work. In their
original form his writings were engraved by a special process he invented.
The plates bear not only words but interinvolved designs, so that design,
poetry, engraving, and sometimes hand coloring combine to offer the
reader a special intimacy with Blake's way of seeing. The passage above
may look rather odd as poetry, but it too is the result of long-meditated art.
At the opening of *Jerusalem*, the poet advises the public that he knows what
he is doing in abandoning rhyme and strict meter. "I therefore have
produced a variety in every line, both of cadences & number of syllables.
Every word and every letter is studied and put into its fit place." The result is a vast corpus of thought, cosmic in its scope and yet punctilious
in every detail of its "minute articulations."

For all these reasons Blake's work has undergone an enormous change
in appreciation. To his contemporaries he was hopelessly obscure. His
poetry went unread except for a few lyrics; his paintings were ridiculed.
He was little regarded except as a talented engraver who suffered from
cranky fanaticism. He earned enough for himself and his wife largely by
accepting disagreeable commissions. But in this century, the depth and
integrity of his vision have been studied and widely admired. He has been
taken seriously on his own terms, as a poet, artist, and even prophet. In the
bleak and violent decades of mid-century he has found not only readers
but converts. Many have grown convinced that he is one of the most
rewarding poets in English since Milton or Shakespeare. Presented with
his choice between materialism and illuminated inspiration, they have
unfolded and shared Blake's visions.

Certainly his bright pages pose a spirited challenge to Jefferson and his
idols. Imagine Blake's scorn for the American minister to France as he
ordered his oval portraits—not at all fussy about the pose or the artist but
planning a simple trio of images: "Bacon at top Locke next then Newton."

Jefferson's letters to Trumbull show him bargaining crassly for any reasonable facsimile. "What would it cost to have them copied by some good young hand, who will do them well and is not of such established reputation as to be dear? Those of Columbus, Vespucius, Cortez, and Magellan [portraits Jefferson had recently ordered from Italy] are well done and cost a guinea and a half each. I do not expect as cheap work in England, tho' I do not expect better." In the end he left Trumbull as his agent to employ whatever copyist to take the lineaments of whatever picture or bust seemed reputably authentic.[15]

And the idea of reverencing Bacon, Newton, and Locke evidently came to Jefferson in a blur. He learned to read them, but not to notice what other worshipers emphasized—that these three thinkers were all great Englishmen. Voltaire's discussion of them was at the core of a book about England. D'Alembert linked them with Descartes, but also stressed the growth of their thought in a climate free of Continental religious repression. Blake was emphatic about nationality. Modern thought had spread its pall over Albion, the ancient name for England. The darkness had spread outward to Europe and the world. Blake saw himself as an English prophet, inspired to attack Bacon, Newton, and Locke on their own ground and to rebuild Jerusalem at the present center of the world, which was where Blake lived in London. By ignoring this national identity, Jefferson was betrayed by it, even in his little anecdote. When he faulted Hamilton and Adams for swerving toward the British constitution, he proclaimed his own devotion to these model British minds!

Yet Jefferson's philosophical and political ideals were larger than some of his own remarks about them. In the Revolution they became so impressive that even Blake admired and celebrated them. A few years ago David Erdman made the convincing suggestion that a passage in Blake's poetry refigures some of Jefferson's famous words (Erdman, pp. 24–25). The first poem that Blake described as a "prophecy" was *America* (1793), in which he saw the American Revolution as a rebirth of mind against tyranny. Plate 6 of the poem combines imagery of resurrection and emancipation with terms from the Declaration of Independence: *life* (lines 1–4), *liberty* (5–11), and the *pursuit of happiness* (6, 8–14).

15. Jefferson, *Papers*, ed. Boyd, 14:467–68, 561.

The morning comes, the night decays, the watchmen leave their stations;
The grave is burst, the spices shed, the linen wrapped up;
The bones of death, the cov'ring clay, the sinews shrunk & dry'd
Reviving shake, inspiring move, breathing, awakening,
Spring like redeemed captives when their bonds & bars are burst.
Let the slave grinding at the mill run out into the field,
Let him look up into the heavens & laugh in the bright air;
Let the inchained soul, shut up in darkness and in sighing,
Whose face has never seen a smile in thirty weary years,
Rise and look out; his chains are loose, his dungeon doors are open;
And let his wife and children return from the oppressor's scourge.

They look behind at every step & believe it is a dream,
Singing, "The Sun has left his blackness & has found a fresher morning,
And the fair Moon rejoices in the clear & cloudless night;
For Empire is no more, and now the Lion & Wolf shall cease."

This is a ringing passage in Blake's work. Phrases from this plate often recur in his later writings. They also stand out in the epigraph of his famous print, sometimes called "Glad Day," a nude with limbs outstretched in a burst of light: "Albion rose from where he labourd at the Mill with Slaves / Giving himself for the Nations he danc'd the dance of Eternal Death."

The joy of these lines rises from many sources. Not least is the immediate hope and confidence of this era of revolution. To Blake, the revolutionaries were doing as a people what he alone had been crying to do in his art. He might refigure Jefferson's words, but he could not outreach their public significance.

Indeed the Declaration of Independence can be understood as a shining public poem of a kind that Blake aspired to produce. It was certainly not by choice that he had become a minor engraver and crank and that he labored alone. His pages burn with the desire to inspire multitudes. As late as 1809 he was preparing a great exhibition of his works, which would draw attention to a scheme for producing huge frescoes in public buildings throughout the land. For another decade he labored over his *Jerusalem*. But few came to his exhibition and no one bought his book. A life spent in such frustration takes its toll. As many critics have remarked, Blake does look deep into the past, present, and future all at once. He seems to have written in the faith that *someday* he would be heeded. And to sustain that faith he made poetry out of deep resources; his passages became intelligible only through long familiarity with the Bible and Milton and the details of Blake's personal life. His great conception is of a universe coming alive; the giant Albion is not only a personification of all mankind but a figure of God, man, and all creation in eternity. But that giant (who sometimes merges with the poet) is imagined as one man all alone, except for other gigantic beings that exist within him.

Jefferson is at the opposite extreme. He was the man singled out to write the common declaration of a revolutionary Congress. While still in his early thirties he thus became the penman who gave verbal form to the destiny of a continent. Among the people of America, the familiar phrases of democracy are still his words or Lincoln's, and Lincoln's depend on Jefferson's. "Four score and seven years ago" is an invocation from 1863 back to 1776 and the self-evident modern truth that all men are created equal. The long span of Jefferson's career encompassed dozens of effective, concerted efforts—congresses, state assemblies, committees, joint commissions abroad, cabinets, political parties, learned societies, networks of correspondence—in which he touched and organized other minds. Like Blake, he labored for freedom from tyranny, for human equality, for universal brotherhood. But he lived and moved and had his being in a new world, where such idealism could be a social reality. Blake re-created America in poetry and art, and yearned for a social awakening; Jefferson lived in an awakening America and found ways to bend European thought and art to the form of his compatriots' energies.

Jefferson therefore emerges as a man far larger than someone caught in the cogs of Newton or dazed in the looms of Locke. In the declaration he absorbed Locke—not the symbol but the political thinker—into a merging of language and action that could inspire, of all people, William Blake!

What remains to be said is that Jefferson's anecdote about himself, the portraits, and Hamilton has its own significant literary form. It is not necessarily fictitious, but it does bear comparison with stories of a certain type.

Jefferson tells a similar story in the 1818 introduction to his *Anas*, only a few pages from another version of the anecdote about Hamilton, Adams, and the British Constitution.[16] This story describes the general mood of the American government when Jefferson returned from France and became secretary of state. He found himself in New York in 1790, surprised and uncomfortable at a succession of dinner parties:

> I had left France in the first year of her revolution, in the fervor of natural rights, and zeal for reformation. My conscientious devotion to these rights could not be heightened, but it had been aroused and excited by daily exercise. The President received me cordially, and my colleagues and the circle of principal citizens apparently with welcome. The courtesies of dinner parties given me, as a stranger newly arrived among them, placed me at once in their familiar society. But I cannot describe the wonder and mortification with which the table conversations filled me. Politics were the chief topic, and a preference of kingly over republican government was evidently the favorite sentiment. An apostate I could not be, nor yet a hypocrite; and I found myself, for the most part, the only advocate on the republican side of the question, unless among the guests there chanced to be some member of that party from the legislative Houses. (*WTJ*, 1:159–60)

In other words, Jefferson often dined with cabinet colleagues and principal citizens and often witnessed a conflict between monarchists and rational republicans. This quotation reveals that he framed memories of this time in a regular pattern, by focusing on dinner parties. As secretary of state he could readily observe the government and its moods in a variety of ways. But his imagination dwelled on social conversations. In this story he again appears as primus inter pares: the president receives him cordially; the outer circles of colleagues and citizens offer welcome. Immediately he moves to the center of familiar society, where he becomes the

16. The other version of the Hamilton-Adams story is in *WTJ*, 1:165–66. It is odd that Jefferson does *not* repeat the story of Hamilton before the portraits, even though here he is writing about Hamilton's character. "But Hamilton was not only a monarchist, but for a monarchy based on corruption. In proof of this I will relate an anecdote, for the truth of which I attest the God who made me" (1:165).

lonely champion of republican thought. There may be some historical truth in such a pattern. Jefferson was a Virginia gentleman newly returned from Paris. The tone of New York dinners may have caught his special interest while, as an experienced politician, he was listening for unguarded disclosures among his associates. Still, there is a congruence between the patterns here and in the anecdote of the portraits; the similarity could not be more striking if they had been written in iambic couplets.

The pattern is the time-worn story of philosophers at a banquet. The most celebrated example is the *Symposium* of Plato, though there were many others to be found in the eighteenth century and in Jefferson's library. Boswell's *Life of Johnson* is full of analogous scenes, in the form of recollections of actual evenings. It may sound odd to call such records a work of imagination, but that is what they are. Boswell, like Plato, recreates idealized heroic dialogues; and so does anyone who plans or recalls a splendid formal dinner. A small elite group gathers at a table, and eventually the blandishments of food, wine, and entertainment give way to an exchange of ideas. So Jefferson introduces his story of the portraits: "I invited them to dine with me, and after dinner, sitting at our wine, having settled our question, other conversation came on." What follows is dialogue that comes to a climax in an overwhelming question. Plato presents a series of speeches on love, culminating in Socrates' revelation of its mysteries. Jefferson narrates a collision on the merits of the British Constitution, followed by his naming the greatest men who ever lived.

The fabric of such stories is obviously social. The private setting and physical comforts guarantee that everyone will be included in good fellowship, even though it is the character of philosophers to disagree. As their discussion becomes more acute, their common civility becomes more remarkable. Dr. Johnson is notorious for verbally trouncing his evening companions, including Boswell, and yet maintaining devoted friendships through the years. Plato seats Socrates at the same symposium with a scoffing Aristophanes and a drunken Alcibiades. The Last Supper of the Gospels brings the disciples together for a ritual feast, where Judas is gently revealed as a traitor and Peter is warned that even he will fall away before the cock crows. So in Jefferson's anecdote: he faces his archenemy Hamilton, who would render up everything to a Caesar, and towers over him among Bacon, Newton, and Locke.

Jefferson's story is hardly a work of literature. It is a paragraph from a self-justifying letter, in which the narrator figures as both host and hero of the tale. But this story unwittingly reveals the strengths that Jefferson prized in his own character. Blake keeps returning to a vision of humanity as a giant who is awakening, stretching, and casting off the nightmares of space and time, science and history. Jefferson does nothing of the sort. He built his dwelling firmly in space and time—to enter Monticello, one must still pass under a compass and an enormous clock! But in this story and elsewhere he views himself as part of a learned society, brightening this world with mutual illumination, in places well furnished with monuments of other explorers and philosophers.

The Assertive Chief Justice

Marbury v. Madison is rightly considered a cornerstone case in American constitutional law. It was the first exercise of judicial review in which the Supreme Court set aside a law made by Congress. It also provided a considered argument to justify using this power, which is not explicitly granted to the judiciary by the Constitution. John Marshall delivered this decision in February 1803. He wrote on behalf of a unanimous Court, but he knew he was taking an enormous step on his own. He was setting a precedent, asserting his full authority as chief justice, and raising the Court to its present status as the final arbiter between the Constitution and legislation. He was also executing an exciting political maneuver, responding to a Jeffersonian plan of government he hated. Finally, he was creating a new way of understanding the Constitution. He asserted that the Court must have the final say over what that document means—that the Constitution must rest in the keeping of a few wise scholars rather than being directly controlled by the people or their representatives.

Marshall's meaning, and the background of his decision, deserve fresh consideration. Even without legal training, one can appreciate the issues involved here. Indeed the legal questions are inseparable from problems of politics, history, and human character and conflict. And, as it happens, the intricacies of all these matters can be seen in depth against a case with a similar cluster of issues, tensions, and personalities.

Almost two centuries earlier, another case, decided by another great and famous justice, had claimed that courts must sometimes declare laws void when they conflict with a constitution. As we have seen earlier, it was on this point that James Otis and John Adams grounded their protests against Parliament: whether fundamental law or parliamentary supremacy was to prevail. It was on a related point—who is to be the judge?—that John Adams and Daniel Leonard rehearsed the issues of the Revolution. In 1803 these questions were still at issue. The early seventeenth-century doctrines of Sir Edward Coke, in *Dr. Bonham's Case*, were to echo in Marshall's decision and in all subsequent American law.

It is impossible to trace exactly how Marshall absorbed Coke's idea. It doubtless came to him through many intermediary sources: modified in law books like Blackstone's, reworked in many pamphlets of the American Revolution including *Novanglus* and *Massachusettensis*, and raised again in debates over the Constitution during its ratification and after. Marshall may never have studied *Bonham* directly, but when the two cases are compared, one sees two strong-willed jurists wrestling with similar legal and political problems. The comparison shows Marshall's thought and character in sharp relief at the outset of his judicial career.

Both cases are famous, complex, and hence encrusted with layers of minute commentary. But one may approach them more simply by describing five leading points of comparison: (1) both cases stated the principle of judicial review—that courts may review laws passed by a legislature and judge them void in certain cases; (2) both cases arose from individuals' grievances, which would be trivial except for this larger principle; (3) both were cases seized on by judges recently appointed to a high bench and decided in an atmosphere of tension after a recent change of regime; (4) both decisions displayed such elaborate reasoning that essential doctrines were buried in sections that could seem extraneous or mere dictum; and (5) both decisions became well-known points of dispute between the justices and their antagonists. Further points of comparison could be explored, but these will suffice to sketch the main issues and the hard political problems each justice addressed.

Coke stated the principle of judicial review in language that echoes in the *Marbury* decision. "And it appears in our books," he wrote, "that in many cases, the common law will controul acts of Parliament, and sometimes adjudge them to be utterly void: for when an act of Parliament is against common right and reason, or repugnant, or impossible to be performed, the common law will controul it, and adjudge such act to be void."[1] These words do not mean what they may seem to mean to a modern reader. Most legal historians agree that judicial review as we know it would have been inconceivable in 1610. What Coke was saying was that judges might control certain laws in particular cases—if they could not be enforced or if their application would result in unforeseen and manifest absurdity. It certainly did not occur to him that courts should be established as tribunals to weigh the validity of parliamentary acts and declare them valid or invalid in all cases.

But two centuries later, many of his words were repeated by Marshall in just such a doctrine: "Certainly all those who have framed written constitutions contemplate them as forming the fundamental and paramount law of the nation, and consequently the theory of every such government must be, that an act of the legislature, repugnant to the constitution, is void." Marshall went on to argue that it is "of the essence of judicial duty" for courts to decide cases where the Constitution and a particular law conflict. And he concluded that the Constitution empowers judges to set ordinary acts aside in such a case. "If then the courts are to regard the constitution; and the constitution is superior to any ordinary act of the legislature; the constitution and not such ordinary act, must govern the case to which they both apply."[2] Despite the great differences between the two cases, their similar wording indicates a common pattern. An act of a legislature, if it conflicts with a more fundamental law, can be held void or of no force, and a law court is the proper agency for making that decision.

These doctrines were stated in decisions in cases that were otherwise unimportant. One concerned a London doctor who was being persecuted by the College of Physicians; the other, a District of Columbia magistrate who was unable to obtain his official commission. Neither Dr. Bonham

1. 8 Coke Reports 118 (1610).
2. 1 Cranch 177–178 (1803).

nor Mr. Marbury would now be remembered if each had not provided the occasion for the stating of an important doctrine.

Thomas Bonham was a London physician with a medical degree from Cambridge University. Under a patent confirmed by statutes of Henry VIII, physicians were required to have either a medical degree from Oxford or Cambridge or a license from the College of Physicians in London. The college charged Bonham with practicing without a license, imposed fines, and finally committed him to prison. He ignored their warnings and brought suit for false imprisonment. The statutes turned out to be ambiguous. It was not clear whether all London physicians had to be licensed by the college, degree or no degree. And the college seemed to have two different powers under different clauses: to fine unlicensed doctors at a set rate and to impose unspecified penalties for malpractice. This dispute moved through the courts with various results. When it reached Coke, he stressed a new legal principle. The college was both charging offenders of the statute and judging their cases; what is more, it was keeping a share of the fines it imposed. Thus it had an interest—a direct financial interest—in its own causes and could not make impartial decisions. The statute setting up such a self-interested tribunal therefore ran against a principle of common law—that one may not be a party and a judge in the same cause. Coke decided in favor of Bonham and strongly implied that any penalties imposed directly by the college would be void unless some way were opened for appellate review.

In the American case, William Marbury had been named a justice of the peace for the District of Columbia in the last days of the Adams administration. But his commission had not been delivered before Adams's term expired, and the Jefferson administration refused to give it to him. Other men also failed to receive their appointments, but thought the office of justice of the peace too trivial to pursue. Marbury, however, and three others brought suit to the Supreme Court, seeking a writ of mandamus—a court order directing James Madison, Jefferson's secretary of state, to deliver their commissions. Delicate considerations were involved. Could the Court issue an order to the president or his subordinate? Could it compel the secretary of state to appear and give evidence? Madison ignored the proceedings, and without his evidence it was impossible to prove even that the commissions still existed.

Like Coke, Marshall based his decision on a new idea. He indicated that justice was on Marbury's side, but Marbury nevertheless lost the suit. The Judiciary Act of 1789 specifically gave the Supreme Court the power to issue writs of mandamus, but Marshall ruled that *this* act violated the Constitution. The Constitution had given the Supreme Court only appellate jurisdiction in such a case, and Marshall held that issuing a writ of mandamus was an act of original jurisdiction. "The authority, therefore, given to the supreme court, by the act establishing the judicial courts of the United States, to issue writs of mandamus to public officers, appears not to be warranted by the constitution" (1 Cranch 176). In a single decision, then, Marshall explained the justice of Marbury's case, avoided a direct clash with the executive branch, and gave forceful effect to the power of judicial review.

Clearly both Coke and Marshall had more in mind than rendering sensible decisions to a physician and a would-be justice of the peace. Both had been recently appointed to high judicial posts, and both had just weathered constitutional crises. They were trying, then, to establish their full authority on the bench.

Coke had been named chief justice of the Common Pleas in 1606, just three years after James I came to the throne. By the time the *Bonham* case came before him, he had already shown that he would oppose even the king in interpreting the long traditions of English law. James had arrived from Scotland ready to assert his royal prerogative; Coke was just as prepared to insist that that prerogative had long been limited by specific cases and well-established procedures.

The tension between them erupted in one of the most dramatic scenes of James's reign. It occurred in late 1608, about a year before Coke weighed the *Bonham* case (1610; report published 1611). Disputes between the ecclesiastical and common law courts had led James to call a session at Whitehall, where he heard arguments and prepared to judge personally between these rival jurisdictions. Coke argued that the English king could not judge personally, without the restrictions of law, in any matter.

The records of this confrontation are varied and Coke's own report seems to compress several conferences into one.[3] But it is clear that the

3. The evidence is presented and weighed in Roland G. Usher, "James I and Sir Edward Coke," *English Historical Review* 18 (1903): 664–75.

king was firm in asserting his power to decide legal questions using his
natural reason and his preeminent authority over the courts. Coke insisted
that laws must be decided by judges qualified by long and arduous study.
At the explosive moment, he said something to the effect that kings do not
protect the laws; rather, laws protect the king. At this, James thundered
that such a speech was treasonous and lost control of himself. According to
one witness, he stopped short of threatening Coke only because the Lord
Treasurer came between them on his knees.[4] According to another:

> His Majestie fell into that high indignation as the like was neuer
> knowne in him, looking and speaking fiercely with bended fist, offer-
> ing to strike him etc., which the lo. Cooke perceauing fell flatt on all
> fower; humbly beseeching his Majestie to take compassion on him
> and to pardon him, if he thought zeale had gone beyond his dutie and
> allegiance. His Majesty not herewith contented, continued his indig-
> nation. Whereuppon the Lo. Treasurer, the lo. Cookes unckle by
> marriage, kneeled downe before his Majestie and prayed him to be
> favourable.[5]

A king offering violence with his bare fist, a chief justice fallen to the
floor: what a scene! Later, when Coke recorded the incident, he elaborated
on it to make a coherent statement of his position, citing precedents and
concluding with a line from Bracton:

> Then the King said, that he thought the Law was founded upon
> Reason, and that he and others had Reason, as well as the Judges: To
> which it was answered by me, that true it was, that God had endowed
> his Majesty with excellent Science, and great Endowments of Nature,
> but his Majesty was not learned in the Laws of his Realm of *England*,
> and Causes which concern the Life, or Inheritance, or Goods, or
> Fortunes of his Subjects, they are not to be decided by natural Rea-
> son, but by the artificial Reason and Judgment of the Law, which Law
> is an Act which requires long Study and Experience, before that a
> Man can attain to the Cognizance of it; and that the Law was the
> Golden Met-wand [measuring rod] and Measure to try the Causes of
> the Subjects; and which protected his Majesty in Safety and Peace:

4. John Hercy to the Earl of Shrewsbury, quoted in Usher, p. 669.
5. Sir Rafe Boswell to Dr. Milbourne, quoted in Usher, p. 670.

With which the King was greatly offended, and said, that then he should be under the Law, which was Treason to affirm, as he said; to which I said, that *Bracton* saith, *Quod Rex non debet esse sub homine, sed sub Deo & Lege.*[6]

Here as elsewhere Coke left a ringing statement of principle: that established law could limit the power even of parliaments or kings, and that the interpretation of that law was the exclusive province of learned judges.

Marshall stepped into *Marbury* fully aware that he, too, was treading on dangerous ground. He had been appointed only recently, in 1801 near the end of Adams's term as president. And in Thomas Jefferson he saw an adversary reckless with power. Adams had deliberately filled the judiciary with Federalists in order to limit the chaos he feared from the Republican sweep in the election of 1800. Marshall shared his fears, and soon he had good reason. While Jefferson withheld commissions from men like Marbury, the Congress proceeded to go after more important prey. It repealed the Judiciary Act of 1801, thereby removing from the bench sixteen circuit court judges who had just been appointed for life. It reorganized the terms of the Supreme Court, mainly so that the repeal would be solidly in force before it could be declared invalid. It initiated proceedings of impeachment for high crimes and misdemeanors against a Vermont judge who was not criminal but manifestly insane. Once that was accomplished (in 1804), it began proceedings against a Supreme Court justice, Samuel Chase.

Nor was this all. *Marbury* was first argued in 1801, but was delayed while Madison was served with a preliminary order to show cause against a mandamus. Meanwhile, Congress delayed the next term of the Court until 1803, and congressional debates echoed with outrage that the Court had served papers on Madison at all. Whether the courts could declare laws void became a matter of loud dispute among lawyers, legislators, and partisan editors. And some Republicans openly avowed that judges should be impeached for no other fault than voicing objectionable views on the bench.[7]

6. 12 Coke Reports 64–65. As Usher notes (p. 665), this account was first published in 1656, long after Coke's death and the seizure of his papers; its relation to Coke's original records is impossible to trace.

7. Despite its pro-Marshall bias, Albert J. Beveridge, *The Life of John Marshall*, vol. 3 (Boston: Houghton, Mifflin, 1919) still provides an amply documented survey of these controversies; it is balanced by the researches of Dumas Malone, *Jefferson and His Time*, vol. 4 (Boston: Little, Brown, 1970).

To Federalists like Marshall and Chase, it seemed that constitutional government was threatened. The 1803 term was sure to bring a crisis. If the Court declared an act of Congress void or gave a direct order to Madison, who could foresee the outcome? Either decision might be ignored or circumvented, or used to justify new curbs on federal judges. Yet the Court dared not retreat, either, and seem to be intimidated by the other branches of government. Jefferson did not literally raise his fist while Marshall dropped to the floor, but the new Republican administration was sure to oppose strongly an entirely Federalist judiciary. The courts seemed doomed to lose more of their weakened authority.

To act effectively against their respective dangers both Coke and Marshall constructed ingenious, not to say brilliant decisions. They affirmed contentious doctrines in the midst of decisions that could hardly be protested. And they wove their reasoning into such patterns of logical subordination that even the hardiest and most acute adversary might wonder how to take exception.

The famous passage in *Bonham* occurs in two forms. In pronouncing his decision, Coke dealt with the statutes that gave powers to the College of Physicians. He did not declare them void; he reasoned from a close reading of their provisions that they could not empower the college to act as prosecutor, judge, and receiver of fines in cases of unlicensed practice. He mentioned a general principle that in some cases—especially where one man would be both judge and party in the same cause—even statute law had been held void. He used the word *void* three or four times. But if *Bonham* is an example of what he meant, then it is hard to fault him for doing anything new. He interpreted a statute strictly and thus eliminated (or voided) the improper loose construction that the College of Physicians had been relying on.[8] Later, Coke rewrote his opinion for publication in the eighth part of his *Reports*. Here he elaborated his reasoning on the bench and penned the famous passage: "that in many cases, the common law will controul Acts of Parliament, and sometimes adjudge them to be utterly void." But if he meant to be provocative by publication, he placed these words in an excellent camouflage. They occur in the fourth of five

8. The decision was reported independently of Coke in 2 Brownlow and Goldesborough, 255, and in a manuscript printed and discussed in Charles M. Gray, "Bonham's Case Reviewed," *Proceedings of the American Philosophical Society*, 116 (1972): 35–58.

reasons given to justify strict interpretation of the clause empowering the college to assess fines on unlicensed physicians but not directly imprison them. The words, that is, were in fine print. One has to magnify them out of proportion to their place in this case in order to make much of them. Many readers have interpreted them to be part of a coordinate reason (one out of five) in this case, and thus to be a mere aside from the bench, a dictum that need have no bearing on this case or any other. An expert reading that sees the fourth reason as part of a tight logical sequence still concludes that it is essential to an act of limited statutory interpretation, not broad judicial review.[9]

Thus, in *Bonham*, now you see it, now you don't. Coke's long and energetic battles against the Stuarts on the bench, in his writings, and later in Parliament suggest that he used this case to assert large powers for the courts. Yet to this day it is impossible to prove that he was not simply making a penetrating analysis of the facts and laws before him according to precise but ordinary rules of legal interpretation.

Marbury v. *Madison* is similarly peculiar in its form. Marshall's opinion opens by stating three questions the Court must answer, and he proceeds to answer them in this order: "1st. Has the applicant a right to the commission he demands?" The Court affirms that Marbury does indeed have a right to his commission. "2ndly. If he has a right, and that right has been violated, do the laws of his country afford him a remedy?" Again the Court affirms the justice of Marbury's plea and the competence of the federal courts to deal with it. "3rdly. If they do afford him a remedy, is it a *mandamus* issuing from this court?" Again the Court affirms Marbury's argument: a mandamus is the proper writ for a case like this. But, at the very end, the Court determines that the Supreme Court cannot issue such a writ, indeed that Marbury lacks proper standing for bringing his case in the first place. In rhetorical effect it is as if Marshall had laid on the bench a pistol named Mandamus, cocked the weapon, aimed it at Madison, narrowed his eyes, and then set it aside, declaring that it wasn't properly loaded and he could never get a license for it.

9. See Samuel E. Thorne, "The Constitution and the Courts: Re-examination of the Famous Case of Dr. Bonham," in Conyers Read, ed., *The Constitution Reconsidered* (New York: Columbia University Press, 1938), pp. 15–24; R. A. MacKay, "Coke—Parliamentary Sovereignty or the Supremacy of the Law?" *Michigan Law Review* 22 (1924): 230.

Again it could be argued that much of this opinion is mere dictum. Only the last part bears on the actual holding, that Marbury cannot obtain a mandamus directly from the Supreme Court; the rest is beside the point. In fact, since Marshall evidently knew what this final determination would be, it has been argued that he should have stated just that and no more.[10]

Even so, what dictum! It is a marvelous diversionary tactic. It plays on all the Republicans' fears of courts giving orders directly to the president or his officers. But then it stops short. Instead it finds one narrow legal loophole—merely the actual exercise of judicial review.

Furthermore, the earlier parts of this decision can fairly be read as integral to the final holding. They explain the deeper issues that had been raised in the pleadings of the case and make important discriminations about how far courts can reach into the operations of the other branches of government. The opinion as a whole is thus a cautious, statesmanlike review of what issues are necessarily political or executive and therefore out of reach of the courts, as well as what laws can and cannot be made by Congress under the Constitution. In other words, the opinion may rightly move in the order it does to specify that the courts can supply remedies to grievances against the federal government, but that judicial review, not mandamus, is the proper constitutional instrument for the judiciary to use.[11]

In any case, *Marbury* left the Republicans without a rejoinder, nor did it leave the courts or the Federalists unscathed. The Court concluded in favor of Madison, not Marbury, and refused to issue a mandamus even after agreeing there was a patent case for one.[12] Far from indulging in a sweeping act of power, like invalidating the recent repeal of the Judiciary Act of 1801, the Court voided only a limited section of the Judiciary Act of 1789. And there was irony here, for that act had been written by expert lawyers, including Marshall's associate justice William Paterson and the

---

10. Here and elsewhere I have threaded my way through this opinion with the aid of William W. Van Alstyne, "A Critical Guide to Marbury v. Madison," *Duke Law Journal* 1969 (1969): 1–47.

11. George Lee Haskins, *Foundations of Power: John Marshall, 1801–1815*, Oliver Wendell Holmes Devise History of the Supreme Court of the United States, vol. 2 (New York and London: Macmillan, 1981), pp. 193–196.

12. Even if by some fluke Madison or Marbury still wanted to make a federal case of their dispute, it was sure to become moot before it was finally resolved. The case would have had to go to a district court and then probably on to the Supreme Court again—and the long-lost commission would surely have expired by then.

former chief justice, Oliver Ellsworth. The voided section had added such powers as mandamus to those already granted to the Court by the Constitution, and Marshall had to strain the wording of the Constitution to reject such an enlargement of authority. Finally, the Marshall Court, having declared one federal law unconstitutional, never ventured to exercise that power again. For decades one could find a precedent in *Marbury*, but it was a precedent without results.

Nonetheless, these two statements of judicial power touched off lasting disputes. Coke's words were repeated and challenged and were cited at his removal from the bench. Marshall's opinion nettled Jefferson to the end of his days.

Soon after it was published Coke's pronouncement became well known as a dangerous and contagious doctrine. It was repeated as common knowledge by Chief Justice Hobart as early as 1614: "Even an Act of Parliament, made against Natural Equity, as to make a Man Judge in his own Case, is void in itself, for *Jura naturae sunt immutabilia* and they are *leges legum*."[13] Two years later Coke was suspended from the bench and ordered to correct his *Reports*; the *Bonham* doctrine was among five specific errors pointed out to him. Coke replied by repeating exactly what he had reported and claiming that this was sound law.[14] Lord Chancellor Ellesmere appears to have written a formal critique of this case, and he sneered at Coke when he was finally replaced on the bench by another chief justice (1616). Ellesmere pointed out the virtues of an earlier predecessor: "He challenged not power for the Judges of this Court to correct all misdemeanours as well extrajudicial as judicial, nor to have power to judge Statutes and Acts of Parliament void, if they conceived them to be against common right and reason; but left the King and the Parliament to judge what was common right and reason."[15] Coke's words nevertheless crept into legal deliberations long after he had been publicly disgraced. His *Institutes* and *Reports* preserved his authority as an oracle of the law, and the principles of *Bonham* were still being weighed seriously in English cases as late as 1871.[16]

13. *Day* v. *Savadge*, Hobart, 85, quoted in Theodore F. T. Plucknett, "Bonham's Case and Judicial Review," *Harvard Law Review* 40 (1926): 49.

14. Plucknett, pp. 50–51.

15. Moore (K. B.), 828, quoted in J. W. Gough, *Fundamental Law in English Constitutional History* (Oxford: Clarendon Press, 1955), pp. 37–38.

16. Plucknett, pp. 58–59.

Marshall's decision in *Marbury* also had immediate effect. In 1804 Jefferson exchanged letters on the subject with Abigail Adams. Here and later, he held that judges should not have sole determination of whether or not a law was constitutional. "You seem to think it devolved upon the judges to decide on the validity of the sedition law. But nothing in the constitution has given them a right to decide for the executive, more than to the Executive to decide for them." Indeed Jefferson held that the president,

> believing the law to be unconstitutional, was bound to remit the execution of it; because that power has been confided to him by the constitution. That instrument meant that it's co-ordinate branches should be checks on each other. But the opinion which gives to the judges the right to decide what laws are constitutional, and what not, not only for themselves in their own sphere of action, but for the legislature and executive also in their spheres, would make the judiciary a despotic branch.[17]

In 1807 Jefferson specifically instructed the district attorney who was prosecuting the Burr case to treat the *Marbury* opinion as "extrajudiciary" and to denounce it, if possible, "as not law."[18] As late as 1823, he was still protesting that *Marbury* was "continually cited by bench and bar, as if it were settled law, without any animadversion on its being merely an *obiter* dissertation of the Chief Justice."[19] Jefferson denied and still resented the implication in the first part of Marshall's opinion—that the president had deprived Marbury of his just rights. But the legal issue of who could properly interpret the Constitution also weighed on his mind. To the end he studiously avoided any reference to Marshall or the Supreme Court in plans for training sound American lawyers at the University of Virginia.[20]

17. Jefferson to Abigail Adams, September 11, 1804, in *The Adams-Jefferson Letters*, ed. Lester J. Cappon, 2 vols. (Chapel Hill: University of North Carolina Press, 1959), 1:279. At the beginning of his presidency Jefferson actually prepared a formal declaration (never released) that the Sedition Act signed by Adams was unconstitutional and void. See Malone, 4:154.

18. Jefferson to George Hay, June 2, 1807, in *The Writings of Thomas Jefferson*, ed. Paul Leicester Ford, 10 vols. (New York, 1892–99), 9:53–54; hereafter cited as *WTJ*.

19. Jefferson to Justice William Johnson, June 12, 1823, in *WTJ*, 10:22.

20. See his letter to James Madison, February 27, 1826, *WTJ*, 10:375–78; the Minutes of the Board of Visitors, March 4, 1825, in Andrew A. Lipscomb and Albert Ellery Bergh, eds., *The Writings of Thomas Jefferson*, 20 vols. (Washington, D.C.: Thomas Jefferson Memorial Association, 1903–04), 19:460–61.

The evidence set out so far may leave an impression of Marshall and Coke as brave and heroic judges, founders of a new line of legal reasoning and defenders of an independent judiciary against the threats of arbitrary rule. And so they have often been revered. But when compared closely, they also reveal themselves as complicated and fallible human beings. There is no denying their contribution to the ideas of freedom under law which still inspire modern courts. But in both men there is a strain of risky boldness that must be acknowledged.

In the first place, ascribing heroism to them as judges is ironic: they both insisted that they were not personal or political leaders, but well disciplined interpreters of good and sufficient laws. Coke made his judgment not out of a claim to personal wisdom but out of sound and learned reasoning from prior cases and long-established rules of interpretation. He also delivered his opinion as one judge among many and reported it as one case among hundreds. Marshall, too, delivered the opinion of an entire court and couched his holding as the plain consequence of strict reasoning. There was an important difference in the way each judge saw the particular laws before him, but both pointed to law as a massive, intricate body of learning no single man could alter.

Coke often stated that the common law of England was the product of centuries of thought and experience. In facing James at Whitehall he was strengthened by that conviction: law and God were above kings. Coke said it again forcefully in the most famous passage in the *Institutes*:

> And this is another strong argument in law. *Nihil quod est contra rationem est licitum*; for reason is the life of the law, nay the common law itselfe is nothing else but reason; which is to be understood of an artificiall perfection of reason, gotten by long study, observation, and experience, and not of every man's naturall reason; for, *Nemo nascitur artifex*. This legall reason *est summa ratio*. And therefore if all the reason that is dispersed into so many severall heads, were united into one, yet could he not make such a law as the law in *England* is; because by many successions of ages it hath beene fined and refined by an infinite number of grave and learned men, and by long experience growne to such a perfection, for the government of this realme, as the old rule may be justly verified of it, *Neminem oportet esse*

sapientiorem legibus: no man, out of his own private reason, ought to be wiser than the law, which is the perfection of reason.[21]

Christopher Marlowe portrayed Doctor Faustus coming to grief after leaving the study of divinity; Coke doubtless would have faulted him for abandoning the English common law! This passage and others certainly imply that England has an established Constitution. It may grow and change through the efforts of other learned men, but it is preserved in the records of the law. A wise man must devote himself to "long study, observation, and experience" in order to grasp it. He can never hope to change it radically.

Marshall does not invoke such a massive evolutionary body of law; he rather proclaims the new American departure of a compact written Constitution. He turns away from the authority of kings, courts, and learned justices to the authority of the people.

That the people have an original right to establish, for their future government, such principles as, in their opinion, shall most conduce to their own happiness, is the basis, on which the whole American fabric has been erected. The exercise of this original right is a very great exertion; nor can it, nor ought it to be frequently repeated. The principles, therefore, so established, are deemed fundamental. And as the authority, from which they proceed, is supreme, and can seldom act, they are designed to be permanent.

These words are at the heart of the *Marbury* decision. The written Constitution is the permanent expression of the American form of government; it was specifically conceived as an authority above all other lawmaking. "The powers of the legislature are defined, and limited; and that those limits may not be mistaken, or forgotten, the constitution is written" (1 Cranch 176). Yet with these words Marshall too implies that mere men are powerless before the greatest laws. It is not justices but the Constitution that renders a statute void.

Perhaps it is inevitable that these men should look hypocritical or even a shade corrupt in such idealistic pronouncements. It is certain that in

21. Coke on Littleton, 97b (1628).

these cases they were far from being solely constitutional interpreters. They were molding the law with their own hands, and those hands were not quite clean.

Coke, says an expert student of his career, was "an extraordinarily able lawyer, a great judge, and a remarkable parliamentary leader. He was, as well, an unpleasant, hard, grasping, arrogant, and thoroughly difficult man." What is more, his arrogance extended to his behavior on the bench and to his writings. He was bold to assert his own expertise and to enlarge his own power wherever he could. In his legal doctrines he reorganized the law in his own image:

> As a rule of thumb it is well to remember that sentences beginning "For it is an ancient maxim of the common law," followed by one of Coke's spurious Latin maxims, which he could manufacture to fit any occasion and provide with an air of authentic antiquity, are apt to introduce a new departure. Sentences such as "And by these differences and reasons you will better understand your books," or "And so the doubts and diversities in the books well resolved," likewise indicate new law. If I may formulate a theorem of my own, I advance this—the longer the list of authorities reconciled, the greater the divergence from this cases cited.[22]

The list of authorities in *Bonham* has been thoroughly examined—and found ambiguous.[23] And at the core of Coke's reasoning is a deeper problem of logic. His pronouncement about adjudging acts to be void depends on a Latin maxim of the common law: "*aliquis non debet esse Judex in propria causa, imo iniquum est aliquem suae rei esse judicum*; and one cannot be Judge and attorney for any of the parties" (8 Coke Reports 118). Coke held that the College of Physicians was acting improperly as a court because it had a direct interest in the fines it assessed; it was both a party and a judge in the same cause. But does not the same stricture apply to a judge who claims that his court alone has the power to interpret the fundamental laws? Is he not awarding himself the prize of supreme jurisdiction? True, *Bonham* was a case in which Coke originally had no direct

22. Samuel E. Thorne, *Sir Edward Coke, 1552–1952*, Selden Society Lecture (London: Bernard Quaritch, 1957), pp. 4, 7.
23. See MacKay, pp. 223–24; Plucknett, pp. 35–45.

interest; the parties were Dr. Bonham and the college. And perhaps in any case, any judge has an arguable interest (of authority, salary, or career advancement) in claiming jurisdiction. But *Bonham* has an odd cast to it even so. If Coke was using it to enlarge his doctrines that his court (not Parliament, not the Crown, but *his* court) was the final arbiter of valid law, then he might well be accused (as James accused him) of usurping power. He was claiming to be judge of who should be judge and deciding in his own favor—on the paradoxical ground that judges should not judge their own causes![24]

Marshall's involvement in *Marbury* is even murkier. He too claimed the authority of his Court to decide that it was the proper tribunal for constitutional determinations. He too made that claim against the emphatic protests of the other branches of government. And in *Marbury* Marshall was personally involved, also. Marbury's commission had passed through his own hands. He had continued to serve as secretary of state until the end of Adams's administration. He was the officer who should have seen to its delivery in the first place. He might even have been authorized to deliver it in the first hours of Jefferson's term. Certainly his own brother, who had been a clerk in the State Department, was called to testify about the last known whereabouts of the commission and the reasons for its miscarriage.[25] Here is a patent case of conflict of interest. If judges should not judge causes to which they are a party, Marshall should have withdrawn from this case from the outset. Marbury's complaint had its source in Marshall's own negligence, a fact that Marbury's attorneys had to strain to ignore.

Finally, therefore, both these cases draw high constitutional principles out of compromised circumstances. It is not a foregone conclusion that Coke rather than James had justice on his side. Ten years earlier, under a well-loved monarch like Elizabeth, Coke's doctrines against prerogative

24. One can go partway around this seeming paradox. Coke's citations in *Bonham* indicated that a party who was assigned to serve as a judge might appoint a qualified delegate to conduct a fair court. The king appointed judges to preside over causes involving the king; so a landowner should appoint a steward to judge disinterestedly over cases involving the master (see Gray, pp. 44–45). But in a case of constitutional dimensions it is impossible to know who could be a proper judge. Coke denied legitimacy to the king's natural reason; the king denied final authority to this expert judge's artificial reason. Between these two strong wills, strong minds, and strong claims to mastery of the law, who could be delegated to render firm judgment? Lord Chancellor Ellesmere came down against Coke, but of course he could be seen as bowing under the pressure of the king.
25. 1 Cranch 146. Marshall's and Jefferson's accounts of how the commissions were detained are quoted and discussed in Beveridge, 3:124–25, and Malone, 4:144–45.

could never have been asserted so positively. No judge would have dared. And Marshall's holding was long disputed by Jefferson and never repeated by the Marshall Court, even though it was conclusive in Marbury's case.

The best that can be said is that both these cases arose in circumstances unforeseen by the constitutions they tested. The common law Coke had mastered under the Tudors was bound to become a different political safeguard and weapon under the Stuarts, just as the Constitution framed and set in place under the aegis of George Washington was destined to be strained, once rival parties emerged and fought for dominance.

In this light, Marshall's achievement is not that he soundly checked Jefferson nor that he preserved the intentions of the framers. Rather, he acted vigorously and brilliantly to strengthen the judiciary against a vigorous and brilliant president.

Marshall delivered the opinion in *Marbury* when he was forty-seven years old. No one then could know that he would remain a powerful chief justice until he was nearly eighty. Up to this time he had traced a varied career—as a soldier of the Revolution, successful Virginia lawyer, advocate of the Constitution in the ratification debates, special commissioner to France, and secretary of state. His first judicial robes were those of the Supreme Court, and he wore them over the tall, loose-jointed frame of a frontier Virginian. His odd mix of political advantages—Federalist, Virginian, young man of the Revolution—made it conceivable that he might yet be president himself. Here was a potent new force on the bench at just the moment Jefferson moved to attack it.

And if Marshall proved equal to this crisis, it must be conceded that Jefferson was a force to be reckoned with, too. He was not an ogre but a principled antagonist of what he perceived to be judicial abuses. An entirely Federalist federal bench was a danger to American law. It had already been rendered partisan by Adams's end-of-term tinkering and by recent and notorious sedition judgments against Republican politicians. Furthermore, the doctrine of judicial review ran against Jefferson's sense of what was fundamental in American life. Some of his arguments against it still deserve a hearing.

At his best Jefferson argued against making the Constitution a fixed, permanent document assigned to the keeping of a few learned men however wise. In the hands of either Coke or Marshall, this is what judicial review implies. Edward S. Corwin long ago put the problem neatly: "In the last analysis, the doctrine of judicial review involves 'an act of Faith,' to wit, the belief that the judges really know the standing law and that they alone know it."[26] To a progressive democrat like Jefferson, such a thought was absurd. In America legitimate power derives from the people, the living people, who continue to express themselves in state and national elections and other forms of active political life. The Constitution outlines the workings of a national government, provides checks and balances, and gives independence to the legislature, the executive, and the judiciary. But to Jefferson's mind it was improper (and ultimately futile) for any of these branches to claim it held final or supreme authority over the law.

He expressed this view of the Constitution fully in a letter of 1815. A correspondent had asked "whether the judges are invested with exclusive authority to decide on the constitutionality of a law." Jefferson replied that there was "not a word in the Constitution which has given that power to them more than to the executive or legislative branches." Each branch, he explained, must decide what is constitutional within its own sphere of operations. If two branches overlap in their spheres of operations, then they must work out a political solution.

> In general, that branch which is to act ultimately, and without appeal, on any law, is the rightful expositor of the validity of the law, uncontrolled by the opinions of the other co-ordinate authorities. It may be said that contradictory decisions may arise in such a case, and produce inconvenience. This is possible, and is a necessary failing in all human proceedings. Yet the prudence of the public functionaries, and authority of public opinion, will generally produce accommodation.

In this same letter Jefferson sketched a notion that at least teased his imagination—that if one branch must be supreme, it should be the legislature. Constitutionally, "this branch has authority to impeach and punish a member of either of the others acting contrary to its declaration of the sense of the Constitution." And practically, the legislature is most immediately responsible to the people, "there being in the body of the nation a

---

26. Edward S. Corwin, *The Doctrine of Judicial Review, Its Legal and Historical Basis, and Other Essays* (Princeton: Princeton University Press, 1914), p. 63.

control over [members of Congress], which, if expressed by rejection on the subsequent exercise of their elective franchise, enlists public opinion against their exposition, and encourages a judge or executive on a future occasion to adhere to their former opinion."[27]

There is still a tension in American politics stemming from this early struggle.[28] And Jefferson's letters bear witness that *Marbury* was not as definitive in its own time as it may seem now. Must there be a definitive answer? Does Marshall reinforced by Coke express the deepest wisdom about law as a protection against either despotism or raw democracy? The safest, most diplomatic, and most hopeful answer was given by Jefferson in another letter, in 1819: "But you intimate a wish that my opinion should be known [that is, published] on this subject. No, dear Sir, I withdraw from all contest of opinion, and resign everything cheerfully to the generation now in place. They are wiser than we, and their successors will be wiser than they, from the progressive advance of science."[29]

27. Jefferson to W. H. Torrance, June 11, 1815, in Lipscomb and Bergh, 14:303–05.
28. A modern critique of judicial review, along Jeffersonian lines, appears in Van Alstyne, esp. pp. 22–29, 34–37.
29. Jefferson to Spencer Roane, September 6, 1819, *WTJ*, 10:143.

American Founding

In his final *Novanglus* paper John Adams drew an idealized portrait of the founders of Massachusetts. He looked to the Puritans who brought the Massachusetts Bay Company with them to America in 1630, and he claimed they knew very well what they were about. They had thoroughly discussed the move before they left their homeland. They came well aware of their rights as Englishmen. These were sensible, well-informed, farseeing people, who came with their charter in their hands: "not the rascally Rabble of Romulus but Gentlemen of Family, Fortune, Education, and Figure."[1]

Here, in one alliterative phrase, is a well-balanced attitude toward American forebears. Adams traces his ancestry to founders who suit his own image as civilized, high-minded men. He appeals to their example in the face of the crisis around him in 1775. Most important of all, he sees them as living people—not legendary followers of a son of Mars driven by fate to survive in a wilderness, but ordinary mortals distinguished by intelligence and strong character, capable of carrying a special law overseas and consciously transforming it to their needs.

There is always an urge toward myth and reverence regarding any founders. A founding is a beginning point in history. Before it, all is chaos

1. *Papers of John Adams*, ed. Robert J. Taylor (Cambridge, Mass.: Harvard University Press, 1977–), 2:383.

or mystery or error or inadequacy; after it, there is order strong enough to last through generations. Figures involved in a founding therefore must seem larger than life. They must know the enduring world better than their successors, for they created its boundaries and did not always live within them. But Adams here both observes and transcends this way of thinking. He sees his ancestors in many different frameworks of history. As a literate eighteenth-century scholar, he may see more widely than they. He contrasts them to the ancient Romans and measures them against the standards of other seventeenth-century Englishmen. They are pioneers on an alien continent, and valuable predecessors for the case at hand. As a result, Adams makes these figures serve his needs. In the *Novanglus* papers he was searching for a fundamental, undeniable principle or precedent. Here his search comes to an end: in men who could hold fast to the old law and make it new.

What Adams sees here is much like what John Trumbull presents in *The Declaration of Independence*. And the same pattern figures in our usual thinking about the founders of the Constitution: a company of responsible, serious men taking the law into their own hands. It is sometimes convenient to think that this scene took place once in the past, under the guidance of a few national leaders. But Adams's appeal to the Puritans introduces a different view. It happened again and again: in 1630, in 1776, in 1787, in 1803. The American founding can be symbolized in one memorable scene, but to an imagination as sophisticated as Adams's, that symbol will not suffice. To the enlightened, scholarly minds of the founders themselves, there was not one select group or even one generation of "founding fathers."[2]

Even the usual handful of representative statesmen are as remarkable for their differences as for their common purpose. The list usually includes Franklin, the first three presidents, Hamilton and Madison, and John Marshall. But as we have seen, these men were various, contrary, and indi-

---

2. My thinking here and throughout this chapter has been influenced by two very different studies of founding and fathers: Hannah Arendt, "What Is Authority?" in *Between Past and Future*, 2d ed. (New York: Viking, 1968), pp. 91–141, and Jay Fliegelman, *Prodigals and Pilgrims: The American Revolution against Patriarchal Authority, 1750–1800* (New York: Cambridge University Press, 1982). Arendt's essay traces the idea of authority as a valuable political force—neither persuasion nor tyranny—to the myth of the founding of ancient Rome. Fliegelman documents scores of examples in the eighteenth century of parents raising their children to be their equals rather than their eternal inferiors.

vidually complex. Each lived through several identities: he was born a British subject in the colonies, and by his own efforts he died an American citizen. In his young adulthood, he was surprised by a call to new and enormous tasks. Franklin was running a controversial newspaper in Boston, and then surviving in Philadelphia and London, before he was out of his teens. Adams was pulled out of a brilliant legal career by the Continental Congress. Washington took command of a national army and later of a national government, with little advance preparation. Marshall left a good Virginia law practice to serve in Congress and within a few months was both secretary of state and chief justice. Moreover, these men harbored contrarieties within themselves. The same man might be at once a frontiersman and a Latin scholar, as Marshall was; a professional soldier and a confirmed civilian, like Washington; a rooted local citizen and a cosmopolitan statesman, like Franklin or Adams or Jefferson. Franklin was young when he caught the knack of balancing the aspects of his life in early America. But others learned it, too, and turned it to steady profit in their public careers.

As they shared the labor of creating a new government, they had to allow breathing room for such variety. The American founding was a protracted give-and-take among strong figures from many backgrounds and regions, working together through decades. They were New Englanders, New Yorkers, Philadelphians, Virginians, and Carolinians; tradesmen, large landowners, speculators, and professional men; men long on the land, recent immigrants, and parvenus; profound scholars and sharp opportunists. And we have seen that in controversy the most like-minded men could become polar opposites: do-good Mather against the do-good Franklins; a monarchist Adams against a monarchist Leonard; Hamilton and Madison in collaboration and conflict. In numerous long and unresolvable struggles, they all puzzled over constitutional dilemmas. They often learned by absorbing the ideas of a dangerous adversary.

It is tempting to think that they achieved an indelible founding, a firm framework of government, a clearly written Constitution that still provides for every contingency of politics. But it is more accurate to conclude that they did something very different—they explored abiding questions about constitutional government.

Is there a framework within Anglo-American law for resolving constitutional disputes? Adams lived out one kind of answer—by losing faith in judicial determinations and going on to lead a revolution. John Marshall lived out another—by fighting in a revolution and then going on to assert the complete and final authority of constitutional law.

Did the American Revolution give birth to new principles of government and justice? Jefferson believed that it did and went on in that belief into his eighties. Adams could never be persuaded and argued with Jefferson until he was ninety.

Is ultimate decisive power lodged in one branch of the federal government? Washington and Hamilton asserted this power for the executive in matters of neutrality; yet Madison loudly and cogently denied it. Marshall asserted it for the Court, but against the real threat of Jefferson's strongly reasoned disagreement.

The Constitution is often described as a system of "checks and balances," and so imagined as the mechanism of a huge pendulum clock. It is enormous, impersonal, and self-regulating, and its great ingenious purpose is to control the energies of odd factions and individuals, federal and local authorities, competing branches and agencies, and release them in small clicks and advances to the benefit of society as a whole. But these men and their questions force us to see it differently, and more humanly. For "judiciary" read John Marshall; for "executive" read Thomas Jefferson; or for "executive" read Alexander Hamilton and for "legislative" read James Madison—then the Constitution becomes not a precision instrument of polished clauses but a web of strong and articulate wills, flexed against one another in well-matched conflict. What is more, by imagining the Constitution alive in this way, one can begin to think of it as growing rather than fixed, as still-to-be-founded in essential ways by coming generations.

For varied as they were, these early American patriots were hardly diverse enough. To millions of current citizens, the founders portrayed in Trumbull's panels are not easy kin to claim. They may seem not only distant but narrow and even, in one perspective, repulsive. They were almost exclusively white, middle-aged, prosperous, landowning, Protestant gentlemen. All were deeply familiar with English language, law, and customs. Almost to a man they read Addison in their boyhood and Coke at the start of their careers—sound British models from which they never completely parted. To their age such men were without question the

American body politic. But two centuries have rendered them a limited, inadequate segment of a nation that now spans a continent and touches every culture on the globe.

At best, however, their silhouettes may help us see them with fuller human respect, as forebears who both invite our emulation and suggest a method for surpassing them. They are not and cannot become the legendary heroes of poetry; they are caught forever in reams of their own quarrelsome prose. And as they turned to others for example, so they encourage us to lead lives of wider freedom. They stand before high ideals that they could name or state very plainly, and yet ask to be understood as themselves not enslaved by such patterns. In each of them there beat the heart of a revolutionary, a man who risked death to reject an outworn way of life and help establish a better one. Long after 1776 that daring was still alive in them all. Their common written legacy is the Constitution. They came to possess its every line as a record and testament of what their lives had meant—and hence held tenaciously to their own principles of interpretation. Yet they also knew in their bones what it meant to act extraconstitutionally. When they had the power, they all did it: in the Continental Congress, on the field of battle, in the Philadelphia Convention, in diplomatic missions abroad, in political parties, in the presidency, on the Supreme Court bench. All of them came of age by throwing off the shackles of apprenticeship, tyrannic empire, outworn ideals, limited self-conceptions. They knew how to live up to exalted public identities and then live beyond them in good faith.

One of Lincoln's early speeches contains a wonderful backward glance at this legacy. It is Lincoln's later words that enshrine the men of 1776 as "our fathers." But in 1838 many of the founders were still within living memory. Adams and Jefferson had died in 1826, Marshall in 1835, Madison in 1836. For other young men in Springfield, Illinois, Lincoln prepared an address entitled "The Perpetuation of our Political Institutions." With eloquence he described the passing of the first American generation as a loss of brothers and sons as well as fathers.

I do not mean to say, that the scenes of the revolution are now or ever will be entirely forgotten; but that like every thing else, they must fade upon the memory of the world, and grow more and more dim by the lapse of time. In history, we hope, they will be read of, and recounted, so long as the bible shall be read;—but even granting that they will, their influence cannot be what it heretofore has been. Even then, they cannot be so universally known, nor so vividly felt, as they were by the generation just gone to rest. At the close of that struggle, nearly every adult male had been a participator in some of its scenes. The consequence was, that of those scenes, in the form of a husband, a father, a son or a brother, a living history was to be found in every family—a history bearing the indubitable testimonies of its own authenticity, in the limbs mangled, in the scars of wounds received, in the midst of the very scenes related—a history, too, that could be read and understood alike by all, the wise and the ignorant, the learned and the unlearned. But those histories are gone.[3]

Like Trumbull, Lincoln here tries to arrest the passing of history, the fading of scars, the mournful loss of a time when "every adult male" knew the meaning of the scenes of revolution. Later in the speech he proposes some futile remedies. He would replace the fallen pillars of the past with new pillars of reason against passion, of sound morality and reverence for the Constitution. He exhorts a constant piety to the memory of Washington.

But with a deeper penetration, Lincoln also sees that the accomplishments of the founders contain a danger and a challenge. "I believe it is true, that with the catching, end the pleasures of the chase. This field of glory is harvested, and the crop is already appropriated. But new reapers will arise, and they, too, will seek a field. It is to deny, what the history of the world tells us is true, to suppose that men of ambition and talents will not continue to spring up amongst us." Here Lincoln looks both ways at once—to the founders whose names are already "transferred to counties and cities, and rivers and mountains; . . . to be revered and sung, and toasted through all time," and to new men who will arise to rival if not overthrow them. Who will these men be, and what will be their Constitution?

The question then, is, can that gratification be found in supporting and maintaining an edifice that has been erected by others? Most

---

3. "Address before the Young Men's Lyceum of Springfield, Illinois," in *The Collected Works of Abraham Lincoln*, ed. Roy P. Basler (New Brunswick, N.J.: Rutgers University Press, 1953), 1:115. I have omitted italics, which may not be Lincoln's.

certainly it cannot. Many great and good men sufficiently qualified for any task they should undertake, may ever be found, whose ambition would aspire to nothing beyond a seat in Congress, a gubernatorial or a presidential chair; but such belong not to the family of the lion, or the tribe of the eagle. (Lincoln, pp. 113–14)

Here is the danger intrinsic to American statesmanship. Will there always be a sufficient number of responsible, strong, farseeing men to hold one another in check as the law passes into their hands? If not, a powerful single founder may again arise in history.

What! think you these places would satisfy an Alexander, a Caesar, or a Napoleon? Never! Towering genius disdains a beaten path. It seeks regions hitherto unexplored. It sees no distinction in adding story to story, upon the monuments of fame, erected to the memory of others. It denies that it is glory enough to serve under any chief. It scorns to tread in the footsteps of any predecessor, however illustrious. It thirsts and burns for distinction; and, if possible, it will have it, whether at the expense of emancipating slaves, or enslaving freemen.

Index

Carrington, Edward, 102
Cato. See Addison, Joseph
Cato, Marcus Portius, 70, 74–75, 76, 84; *see also* Addison, Joseph
Cato's Letters, 75
Charles II, 60, 63
Chase, Samuel, 144, 145
Coercive Acts, 43, 44, 45, 49
Coke, Edward, 139–56 passim, 160; on fundamental law, 56–57, 140, 144, 148, 150–51; *Reports,* 140, 145–46, 148, 152; and James I, 142–44; *Institutes,* 148, 150–51
College of Physicians, London, 141, 145, 152–53
Concord, Massachusetts, 47
Congress, United States, 89–90, 92, 93–94. *See also* Continental Congress; Constitution, United States
Constitution, British: revered by New England lawyers, 36–39; Adams and, 39–63 passim, 117–19, 135, 136; Loyalist version, 40–41; to American Patriots, 41; Hutchinson on, 50–51, 56–59; and Hamilton, 105–06, 117–19, 135, 136; Coke on, 150–51, 152–53
Constitution, United States: problems in framing, 42–43; on presidency, 89, 92, 99–106, 149, 154–56, 160; on legislative branch, 101–02, 104–05, 155–56, 160; on judiciary, 138, 140, 142, 144–45, 146, 149, 154–56, 160; on executive branch, 145, 149, 160; source of authority of, 151. *See also* Judicial review
Constitutional Convention, 86, 98, 161
Continental Congress, 66, 68, 79, 123, 161; and John Trumbull, 2, 6, 7, 8–12; as a cause of Revolution, 40, 42, 49, 52; John Adams at, 52–54
Conway, Thomas, 67, 68
Copley, John Singleton, 2, 6
Cornwallis, Charles, 65
Corwin, Edward S., 155
Cosway, Maria, 7
Custis, Martha. *See* Washington, Martha Custis
Custis, Nelly, 13

d'Alembert, Jean Le Rond, 124, 132
Dalrymple, Col., 61
Dante, 70
David, Jacques-Louis, 6
Declaration of Independence (document), 8–9, 13, 60. *See also* Jefferson, Thomas
Declaration of Independence (painting). *See* Trumbull, John
Defoe, Daniel, 28

Dennis, John, 71–72
Descartes, René, 132
Douglass, Dr. William, 25
Dunlap, William, 81
Du Ponceau, Pierre Étienne, 68–69

Elizabeth I, 153–54
Ellesmere, Thomas Egerton, Lord, 148
Ellsworth, Oliver, 148
Erdman, David, 132–33
Ewing, George, 69

Fairfax, George William, 76–77
Fairfax, Sally Cary, 76–77
Farquhar, George, 80
Federalist. See Hamilton, Alexander; Madison, James
Federalist Party, 93, 96, 112, 119–20, 123, 144–45, 147, 154
Fenno, John, 90
Feu de joye, at Valley Forge, 69–70
Fitzpatrick, John C., 77
Franklin, Benjamin, 65, 79, 116, 158–59; and John Trumbull, 7, 8, 12; apprenticeship of, 15–34 passim; *Autobiography,* 16–18, 19, 20, 26, 27, 31, 32; arrival in Philadelphia, 16–18, 19, 32; as "Silence Dogood," 20, 27–31; and Addisonian wit, 20–22, 26–31, 32–34, 36; as "Janus," 32–33; and John Adams, 35–37
Franklin, James: and the *Spectator,* 19, 21–22, 26, 28, 33; and Cotton Mather, 19, 24, 26–27, 28, 32, 159; Benjamin's brother and master, 19, 26, 28, 30, 31–32, 33, 34, 159
Frederick, Prince of Wales, 72, 112
Frederick the Great, 112, 127
Freneau, Philip, 90, 102
French alliance, in American Revolution, 65, 69–70, 103
French Revolution, 2, 100–01, 102, 108, 119, 125, 129, 135

Gates, Horatio, 67, 68, 78
Gazette of the United States, 90, 100, 102, 103
Genêt, Edmond, 106
George II, 72
George III, 41, 63, 72, 83, 112
Gilbert, Felix, 112
Goethe, Johann Wolfgang von, 7
Gordon, Thomas, 75
Gordon, William, 78
Greene, Nathanael, 80
Gridley, Jeremiah, 38, 60, 62
Guardian (journal). *See* Addison, Joseph